YOU ARE A BEAUTIFUL GENIUS
BORN INTO THE WORLD WITH
GIFTS OF LIGHT AND LOVE.

PLEASE OVER-USE THEM!

DEDICATION

To my Mom, who gave life to me and made it possible to write in the first place.

To my mentor, spiritual brother and friend, Dr. Leonard Coldwell. Without his mentorship, guidance and love, this book would not exist.

To all the awakening souls who want to live a better existence filled with a new level of love, dynamic health, abundance and energy.

To those who are hungry for spiritual enlightenment and ways to obtain it.

In service to Mother and Father God and the people,

Thank you! Thank you! Thank you!

Contents

Chapter Three: WELLBEING

Chapter Four: PASSION

Chapter Five: SPIRITUALITY

Chapter Six: LOVE

Section Two

MANIFEST YOUR DESTINY

Chapter Seven: TRUTH

Chapter Eight: SUCCESS

Chapter Fourteen: Fɪғᴛʜ Dɪᴍᴇɴsɪᴏɴ

Chapter Fifteen: Cᴏɴᴄʟᴜsɪᴏɴ

Bᴏɴᴜs: Sᴛɪᴍᴜʟᴀᴛɪᴏɴ

INTRODUCTION

I am excited for you the reader and for myself in finally getting this book out there! The quest within this book is to ignite inner and outer life awakening, growing, ever changing, advancing, becoming more real and continuing in a much better way than ever before. This intro to the book is also an introduction to the Author, as the contents come from my process of growing/waking up. This human life of ours is all about a spiritual experience and is the perfect opportunity for the unfolding of spiritual maturity. As we also grow mentally and emotionally, we gain increasing wisdom and discover more of the truth of who we really are.

There comes a time when being terribly lost without a clue and having the proverbial black cloud over one's head must come to an end. It doesn't matter how screwed up your life has been with a rough childhood or now as an adult. I have learned that our life experiences, no matter how terrible, don't have to shape who we are or who we become. For instance, I personally was in and out of foster homes from about age four to eighteen. I had to overcome tremendous obstacles to bring this book to you! The number one lesson for everybody is:

When you get knocked down, get up again and stand a little taller than you did before until your foundation is unbreakable!!

"Something More"… where is it? I think everybody at one point or another has asked themselves this. Looking up at the stars in wonderment at a very young age is where it all begins. All beings are aware of their surroundings and figure out really quickly something is wrong here on this beautiful planet Earth. There are plenty of indicators, such as: Violence and war, domination and hate, racial profiling and human suppression, working for survival and fighting over resources and or the need for money/debt creation. These things are part of our collective third dimensional consciousness and are no longer necessary as we advance/mature together.

The next thing we do is start adapting to life with our own version of, what I like to call our "Shield for Existence!" This wall of protection comes complete with a very complex array of masks wrapped in ego and personality. Over time, the real you and the innocent inner child/light being gets lost.

So, what are we looking for? What is the true reality? How can we better ourselves? How do we awaken to and find our true self again? Where is the love, joy, grace, morals, compassion, unity we know are the truth behind this existence? The most important question for us all, to ask ourselves is:

How do we break through the false reality that we have created for ourselves and the planet and keep our light shining, never to be hidden under veils of illusion again?

We will explore this thing called life through our own self-realization, together, and find some answers to these questions!

This book you now hold in your hands represents my continuing journey through enlightenment beginning as a little boy to adult man. I have been busy figuring life out, discovering who we really are and how life should truly be for all God's children.

OUR PERSONAL PHOENIX

It is true, there is a phoenix inside all of us. The phoenix represents the child of the past, the adult of the future and the person of the now. Just like the phoenix, the inner child within each of us is back and rising up from the ashes of a burned out, old world/paradigm.

Every person's consciousness is evolving, including Gaia - Mother Earth - or Terra as she prefers to be called. We are being reborn and rejuvenated with a new fire and golden light in our eyes. As awakened conscious light beings, it is high time to " Integrate success into our lives."

This is our progression together as one, moving out of the third dimension (Earth One) and into the fifth dimension (Earth Two) or New Lemuria. As we leave the illusions behind, the old world becomes non relevant to us.

Now, we are creating a beautiful, new, loving world as it should be, with Freedom, Peace, Love and Wealth in every area of life. This is our new paradigm! A new way of existence for all that is long overdue: to live long and prosper while pursuing our goals, dreams and aspirations.

So, the truth should be available to us all! I have pulled together some subjects/topics that I think you will find very interesting. First, we will talk about them and explore the deeper meaning within each one, and then I will provide you with some more information to continue with your own self-realization. We will try to answer some of the questions that are on everybody's mind, in terms of: What do I read? What can I watch? What is good to explore? …and things of this nature.

It is my goal to connect with everybody who wants to listen and is open minded enough to receive not only new knowledge, but also the truth that I have gathered. I wrote this book with the intent to enlighten and empower you in many ways, emotionally, spiritually, mentally and physically!!

I want you to know: You are a very powerful, conscious light hue-being who is absolutely very unique and also very loved. You have free will and nobody has authority over you!!!!

This information will hopefully give you a better idea about what you can do for yourself to invite success in everything you do. My hope is that every one of you can use this knowledge to enrich your life, expand your dreams and pioneer your existence to new heights!

Christopher Link   Jacksonville, Florida

SECTION ONE

INTEGRATE SUCCESS INTO YOUR LIFE

Chapter One

ENERGY

ADJUSTING ENERGY

The true nature of everybody and everything in the **universe/multiverse**, and things we can't even see, is **energy**! All of us have our own unique energy signature. By that I mean your personal energy vibrating at a different frequency than other people and things.

Through my searching, I have found and realized that everything is alive and has consciousness, from people to animals, nature and things that wouldn't even be considered to be alive like rocks, machines or structures. Since all things are giving off energy and vibration, sometimes the field of energy can get distorted. Talking about us as humans, this is where negative energy and influences come into play.

There is a lot we could talk about in terms of energy, but we want to focus on what is causing us to have low/negative energy or a low vibration. Ultimately, the goal for each person is to have a high vibration that is in line with full consciousness and beyond. In some way, shape or form, energy revolves around everything we do and will become. It is the foundational underpinning for our whole existence!

FEAR AND LIES

One of the biggest challenges that affects our energy in a major way, as you know, is **fear**! This very bad negative energy has been one of the main culprits and illusions keeping us in a low vibrational state forever.

So, why have we **(The populace)** been living in fear for so long? People live in fear because they don't have the **truth and knowledge** to understand and deal with life properly. Hence the saying: **"People hate what they fear and fear what they don't understand!"**

We have all been lied to in countless ways, generation after generation. If this wasn't the case, there wouldn't be any fear at all! There wouldn't be any fear because instead of lies we would have the truth and real teachings based on honesty, respect and love.

We want/need loving light energy in every way, not fear and negative/dark energy. Whenever the focus is primarily on fear, doubt and worry, this means there is a major lack of **truth and love**!

You will be happy to know that there isn't any such thing as fear, only created delusions that have been perpetuated. Most **(a high percentile)** of what people think are facts or, you could say, what people have fears about, are just someone else's opinion **(Delusion)** and or lies that they, themselves have been told. This chain of lies has continued throughout time for the purpose of control and manipulation of the masses.

Now you can see how the fear monster got created. This spreads around like wild fire and as the saying goes, FEAR is: **"False Evidence Appearing Real!"** The evidence is fake or false, and man's opinion/adopted belief is appearing real because of endless brainwashing since the beginning of human civilization for the purpose of maintaining power and control over people. Remember, **fear won't be present when truth and love are around!**

BLOCKING THE ENERGY FLOW

When all of this keeps spinning out of control, it doesn't take long to bring out or about the energy blocks that we have and experience. If you and I are thinking and saying to ourselves I need more money, I want better health, or I want a better relationship and love in my life, we are actually saying that we want more and better free flowing energy! These fear-based ideas become thought-forms and over time become deeply held beliefs.

Negative thought- forms like fear, greed and resentment, give us a low vibration and keep us down in a blocked state! We then become angry and we make things worse by hating life and blaming others.

Hate is another energy blocker! If somebody is intensely disliking another person, whatever the reason, it is obvious that the light energy is blocked. If this isn't relieved, it could lead to a negative action like violence or even murder!

Another huge form of energetic blocking is **mysticism**! "This happens when we "**give our power/energy away"** to external or outside sources because we have been deceived into thinking that they can help, guide or direct us in some way.

It doesn't matter if it's governments, religions, corporations or other people. As you have probably figured out and can see, this type of buying into lies and misconception has put the whole planet in a bad way and the continuation of life itself is at risk.

Our personal negative energy blocks us, and if that is combined with negative energy from everybody else, it will block the whole planet from progressing. This is why it has been said that we live in a frequency-sick world or an anti-civilization.

Positive change for progressing forward with growth for us and the planet begins with loving energy!

The good news is that the heavy and dense/negative third dimension we have been a part of and living in for so long now is at a close. Everything that is going on in the world right now, you could say, is growing pains and remnant on our way to higher loving energies and dimensions!

OUT WITH THE OLD, IN WITH THE NEW

What I am alluding to here is the **Golden Age/Age of Aquarius and New Earth** that you have been hearing about. This energetic shift of the **(Old)** ages and time lines will put us in a whole new realm where fear and negativity are non-existent.

As we are **leaving illusions behind** and heading into the **new age**, we want to focus on getting rid of negative baggage and raise our vibrations as much as possible. We will accomplish this by getting the positive **(Ball)** vibration bigger than the negative **(Ball)** vibration! Our ball of energy is like a meter and for the longest time now it has been reading in the negative, the time has come to raise to a higher/ positive level for further advancement. This is already happening, so you can trust that we're on the right track!

WHEN WE ARE READY

You have probably heard the saying: **"When the student is ready, the teacher will appear!"** What does this mean exactly? When we put our energy or vibration out into the universe for what we want or desire the universe starts working with the trillions of variables to bring it to us.

We are all connected and like attracts like, so when you are ready **(The Student)**, the teacher will appear as a person to talk to, a book to read, an audio to listen to or a video to watch.

There is endless variation in the form and manner in which the teacher shows up. It can be anything that you need at that moment to put you on the right path to getting what you are looking for, need, want or desire.

We have access to all kinds of people, websites, stores, books…etc. In this book, I am trying to inform you about the best resources I have found, used and studied. Within this book you will see that a lot of Ideas and topics are interwoven and go along together hand in hand – such as, energy and the next topics we will be talking about.

Talking about energy, we are covering the very basics here. I am trying to establish a root base to start from and then you can just keep going into your own explorations. Throughout the book, we will be exploring how energy relates to our lives, and how to utilize it in a positive fashion for the highest good of ourselves and others.

WHAT CAN I DO FOR BETTER ENERGY?

For starters: The best thing we can do as energy/light beings to increase our vibration in a positive manner is to simply be more loving! We can also raise our energy through a bunch of little things, such as: Laughing a lot, watching movies/comedy shows, exercising or going for walks in nature. Giving is always good, to your favorite charities or helping others in general. Playing with your pets or kids, and of course romantic love, is always good.

I have learned that taking steps to create anything you long for is a huge help, such as music or art. For example, while learning to play the drums, I am finding that the rhythmic beat of drumming is very therapeutic and helps me find my center.

So, playing an instrument or creating music and art can be a big help in raising one's vibrational level, among other creative outlets. Recreational activities, sports and just making time to have fun and enjoy yourself/life with others is also very important.

WHO CAN I LISTEN TO?

www.loveorabove.com   This site has a lot of information on energy blocks and ways to clear them with good knowledge about raising one's vibration.

WHAT BOOKS CAN I READ?

Here are a few good books to read:

See You at the Top (Zig Ziglar, 2005). This book teaches about getting rid of negative thinking in order to move forward and have upward growth.

The Source Field Investigation (David Wilcock, 2012) is full of information about the new science of energy and how it effects everything in the universe.

Ask and It Is Given (Esther & Jerry Hicks, The Teachings of Abraham, 2003) has very good information on how to raise your vibration through different and positive techniques.

Chapter Two

HEALTH

IMPROVEMENT FOCUS

Now that we have established an energetic basis for all of life, we can see that our health ties in with everything. We have lots of things to talk about concerning health, but I wanted to keep the focus on improvement. The goal is to reach **Dynamic Health!**

Notice, if you will, the word **Heal** is in the word **Health**, but what needs to be healed? As you probably have guessed, it is the Energy Body, and you are correct! Our bodies have the ability to naturally heal, but they have to be in good working order to do so. If something is going wrong with the physical body, one can bet that the energy or etheric body is off in some way.

An optimum condition for the body is a high alkaline/oxygen- enriched state. Dr. Leonard Coldwell **(My Mentor)** is one of the best doctors out there, specializing in cancer and helping people by natural and alternative means, with a very high success rate. He talks about how diseases like cancer can't survive in the body when it's in this alkaline state. There will be more information about him in later chapters. For now, let's talk about what is causing all the troubles in the first place.

IDENTIFYING ISSUES

One of the main culprits is bad diet. I personally wasn't eating very well in my younger days, which caused me to have some health issues and weight gain. If we are wanting to "Preserve the sexy," we have to watch what we put in our temple/body vessel, and this I have learned the hard way! But, that's okay, because I can now share with you things to stay away from.

What contributes to a bad diet? Processed/fried food and unnatural food, as in an engineered product. These are at the top of the list, complete with names we can't pronounce.

Some unhealthy food additives you might be familiar with include: Mono-sodium glutamate **(MSG)**, aspartame, sugar, high fructose corn syrup, hydrogenated oils…etc. All of this stuff, along with hormones, pesticides, preservatives and food coloring that is going into the process of making food, is slowly killing us!

When we eat all of this junk in our food, we are consuming all kinds of toxins that are not only bad for the body, but overwhelming it. In turn, this makes us gain weight, be docile and sterile, have low energy and plants the seeds for all kinds of health issues to surface over time.

Another big issue affecting our health and the food we eat is Genetically Modified Organisms (**GMOs**). We will talk more on this topic and its implications for the health of the planet as a whole in a later chapter.

Food isn't the right word for these substances, as it is they are not natural! They are products created in a laboratory that have spread into everything. Our bodies have a hard time trying to process and handle these products, which are altered food devoid of the life force. The rejection of these foreign substances puts major stress on the body's systems, with many forms of "dis-ease" as the result.

STRESS FORMS

Stress is the number one cause of diseases, many of which get their start from a low/negative energy flow and a highly stressed, acidic body. If not alleviated, these conditions can lead to all kinds of health issues and even death!

We experience a snowball effect when we don't pay enough attention to our health and fail to keep ourselves in a positive state. Environmental toxins also contribute to poor health, such as: Heavy metals, chemical/air pollutants, drugs – legal or not, smoking...etc.

Sounds like a huge challenge, right? Don't worry... worrying is negative goal- setting, and we don't want to do that! I have a lot of information to share with you for positive goal-setting on your way to **Dynamic Health**!

Now, we will offer some good things to do and learn about in our questions and answers section. Please remember that trying and doing these things for your health may require a major lifestyle change. I'm sure you will realize, as I did, that you can and deserve to have the best health possible!

Be sure to take things slowly and really explore what you are interested in. Health is also very important for our well-being, which I hope you will join me in talking about next!

WHAT CAN I DO FOR MY HEALTH?

As you have seen and heard, there are many ways to cleanse the body, which is what we want to do first. There are single cleanses like: Colon, liver, gallbladder, heavy metal and kidney, but we want a full body cleanse.

www.qnlabs.com On this site you will find a good whole body cleanse called, **Dragon Cleanse**. It is good to do the cleanse about every six months, or four if possible. After cleaning our bodies out, we don't want to put bad toxins back in, so this is where good eats come into play!

WHAT IS GOOD TO EAT?

It is good, as much as possible, to drink and eat **organic**, fresh/raw foods that are **non-GMO**. You can get organic food at a lot of stores these days, but you want to make sure it has the **USDA** organic seal on it. The region or area you live in is also an important factor. "Buying Locally," can have energetic benefits in terms of compatibility with our bodies. Locally grown produce and vegetables brings you the freshest possible food substance and is also a great way to support the community and local farmers. If you have a personal organic garden, that is even better!

Also, you want to select food and drinks that have labels for **no GMO** or **non-GMO project verified** on it. Another thing to watch out for while you are shopping for good eats is the little sticker labels that you see on fruits and vegetables.

These usually have a five digit code on them with the first number representing what that particular food is. If it has a number four first, it is conventional and made with pesticides and herbicides. Number three or eight means **GMO** and this product has been genetically modified. If it has a number nine, that is organically grown and what we want!

I have found a couple of good **APPs** you can use with your smart phone, if you wish. On these websites: www.fooducate.com and www.buycott.com you can download the APP and pull it up whenever you want to use it.

Both of these have a bar code scanner that will scan the code on any item and tell you about the nutritional value. This is kind of like a health grade, and then it gives you healthy alternative ideas too. So, now that your health is getting better and better, it is good to keep educating yourself and finding healthy things that work for you.

HOW DO I MAINTAIN MY GOOD HEALTH?

On www.foodmatters.com they have a lot of health and nutrition information. A good video to watch is called **Hungry for Change**. They also have a lot of other videos to check out on multiple topics to educate yourself on a healthy lifestyle.

When you are switching to organic foods and becoming more health conscious, the key is to just start integrating it into your life. For example, begin with twenty-five percent at a time, or whatever you are comfortable with – there is no need to rush or pressure yourself. If you are looking to shop online for affordable organic food, check out: www.thegreen-polkadotbox.com.

As we are maintaining our good health, Water, of course, is very important. You want to have good clean water that is fluoride free, or filtered using a system that produces an alkalizing **pH** seven or higher. Seven is neutral, and below seven indicates acidity. The purest water possible is important in more ways than one. Author and scientist Masaru Emoto has done research on how our consciousness can affect the molecular structure of water. We can do this by praying over the water or holding the conscious intent to make it pure and energized. You can explore this further with a film on YouTube intitled, ***Water: The Great Mystery*** or ***The Magic of Water***. Also see Emoto's book ***The Hidden Messages in Water***.

Speaking of water, don't forget to stay hydrated while you are exercising, which, as you know, is also a very good way to stay healthy. You don't need to strain yourself with exercise, just anything that gets the heart pumping and blood flowing for about thirty minutes each day.

After burning up nutrients, we need to replenish. This is where good vitamins come in. Getting our vitamins in the right way is kind of like food in that you want to avoid the ones that have been processed. We want them to be as pure as possible, and organic. You can find top quality vitamins at: www.vitopia.biz. This site sells single or multivitamins, but all are good. Another good website is www.mercola.com. Look under health products/whole food multivitamin.

Chapter Three

WELLBEING

WELLNESS OF THE BEING

Where does passion come from? I have figured out that our passions in life are directly linked with our well-being. Keep in mind that this is also directly proportionate to the health and energy we have.

We can also gauge our well-being with the level of happiness we have. I think it is wise for us all to make happiness our number one goal and to be working on a state of bliss, for the best well-being we could possibly obtain.

As you know, this isn't easy, but it should be. Now, it might not always be peaches and cream, but I believe it's possible for us to make incremental changes that improve our general state of mental and physical health and strive to be consistent. This state of well-being activates an energy field of attraction for everything you are desiring in your heart, and more and more good things start to show up in your life.

Sounds great, right! So, why is it so hard to maintain a happy state of being? Survey results show: Depression/Anxiety and general unhappiness are rampant due to us being very stressed out a lot of the time!

A High stress level causes negative/low energy which turns into bad health and can put you - the light being - in a state of dis-ease or not functioning to your highest capacity.

So, one minute you are a happy camper, in love, enthusiastic and in a state of joy; next minute, back down in the dumps, angry and depressed. Why?

WELLBEING ROLLERCOASTER

You have the highs and the lows and it is hard to stay on the high plane. I call this our well-being emotional rollercoaster ride. I have realized that this ride we go on is a natural part of the journey to find our passions in life and discover, or uncover, who we were meant to be.

Some people recognize their purpose at an early age; it's obvious, out there and easy to see. For others, it is hiding just below the surface and many of us have to devote some time and attention to figure it out.

For example, a person wanting to play guitar and be a musician. Has probably been dreaming about it and playing since age five, imagining him/herself becoming a big rock star. That type of person, if they stick with it, will do just that.

For most of the populace, however, it is very stressful trying to discover our ambitions in life. We go through many jobs, relationships, businesses, schools and training looking for ourselves and our purpose. After a while, stagnation sets in and our well-being takes a big hit. We become bored and burnt out, unsatisfied with our lives, bitter, cold, resentful and unforgiving.

So, what do you think the answer is to maintaining a great and positive state of well-being? I will give you a big clue: STIMULATION! This starts with a source or beginning spark that gets you motivated on the passion path. It is good to keep stimulating yourself with positive and interesting information on what you find to be exciting.

Anyone who is adding a creative value to the planet with what they are passionate about, in some way, shape or form, finds themselves very stimulated.

In turn, this leads to happiness and great sustained well-being! Now for the good stuff! The stimulation is rolling in with the questions below and gets better with the news in the next chapter!

HOW DO I RAISE MY WELL-BEING?

www.drleonardcoldwell.com   On this site you can read about Dr. Coldwell and explore what he has to offer, which is all very good and highly recommended. He has a system he created called **IBMS** or **Instinct Based Medicine System**. This is all about you having the best well-being and health possible!

www.instinctbasedmedicinestore.com   This is where you can find books like: *The Only Answer to Stress, Anxiety and Depression*, *The Only Answer to your Doctor and Your Illness*, *The Only Answer to Cancer*, and other great books by Dr. Coldwell. Also, there are multiple audios available about success, motivation and bringing out the **Champion in you!**

WHO CAN I TALK TO?

www.consciouslifeexpo.com   On this site you will find news for events and workshops that involve many speakers, bringing people together to expand the mind and connect in spirit.

WHAT CAN ASSIST MY WELL-BEING?

www.bestpinksalt.com   This site has multiple varieties of pink salt that is pure **(not processed)**, which can be used to help you detoxify the air and your body, offered in different forms to match your needs. For example: Bath salts, fine salt for cooking, salt lamps for your rooms…etc.

Please remember my intention is to inform everybody about the best information and material/products that I have found through my research and truth seeking. Please do your own research and don't blindly take my advice or word for it.

My wish is that this book and information will assist you with your own research into what you are looking for and what is correct for your personal needs. After you read up on things that interest you, make sure to consult your doctor with your new ideas on the products you would like to try, if you are under a doctor's care.

Chapter Four

PASSION

PASSION IS CURIOUSITY

"I don't have a special talent; I am only passionately curious!" Have you heard somebody say this? Whatever you are curious about and are drawn to explore more deeply – which could be anything under the sun – might lead to developing talents that you become passionate about.

The impulse of curiosity is a constant and is always there; the talent has to be formed. Everybody has passion of one sort or another, for something. The idea is to recognize it in yourself and bring it up and out to the surface through some form of outlet.

Passion arises from learning a skill that you are enthusiastic about, which turns into and brings about a talent or even multiple talents. First comes the gift from God; then you have the drive to do the certain thing or skill you are interested in. Then your work ethic and love for what you are doing turns into a special talent which becomes one of your newly formed passions in life.

UTILIZING GIFTS

Your gifts from God could be multiple things, such as: Drawing/art, patience/ teaching or nurturing/healing. The list could go on and on, but I have found that these gifts might remain dormant or unused if not focused properly toward some kind of pursuit even if it is just a hobby.

The gift alone won't get us where we want to be; it is great by itself, but still needs to be developed. The important thing is to give attention to that special God-given gift so that it will turn into a talent or skill that you can utilize as a tool to lift up and bring happiness to yourself and others.

BREAKING DOWN PASSION

I have a recipe with four parts to it, with one of them being **LOVE**! As you know, love is the underpinning of everything, so we have to make sure it's in there. So, you can set your life up to include key ingredients, kind of like baking a cake.

First, we need to explore and see exactly what **PASSION** truly looks like. Next, we can figure out the ingredients so everybody will know and understand the formula. After awareness on a personal level it will make it easier for you to spot talents, gifts and passions in others.

What are you truly interested in? Now, since this can vary greatly, we have to look at things we find ourselves naturally drawn to in our free time, such as hobbies outside of your job that you find yourself doing a lot.

Whatever it is, this might be a passion or the start of one. For example, it's the weekend and instead of going out with your friends, you're at home making creative animal figures with the technique of glass blowing.

Now, your regular job to pay the bills may be taking care of things, but it's a lot of work and creates stress in your being. Working at this particular job is also taking up too much time, so you feel deprived of what you really enjoy doing. In short, it isn't what you are passionate about.

If you are doing something that you truly love and really enjoy, you are having fun, you're happy and best of all, you aren't concerned with how much time it's taking up. So, with our example here, we can put all the pieces together – the ingredients, if you will – for our passion recipe.

FORMING THE PASSION

One of your gifts from God might be art, to be expressed how you choose in many different possible ways. For example, the talent in glass blowing is formed through your love for animals. After you practice and hone your skills, you can eventually be a professional glass blower and sell your art. This is what you would be truly passionate about if that were the case.

Everybody can utilize this simple formula for anything and everything in bringing out their true passions. Now you can start doing what you truly want to do in life! I have noticed that there is a huge difference between doing what you are passionate about and routine work at a job you aren't really interested in. We will talk more in detail about work in a later chapter also. For now, why is this so?

When we create something that gives somebody else joy and happiness, it in turn gives us a great feeling. This is because we have created a value for society and nobody can take that away. Have you noticed that people who are passionate about something have a certain flare about them? They are interesting and attractive, not to mention happy and joyful!

Sometimes it's easier to notice a passion in somebody else and it can be more difficult to see our own. For instance, you might have a friend or relative who seem to be really happy when they are cooking. You notice this and mention to them that they have great skills, the food is delicious, and that they should open up their own restaurant or catering service.

Something else you might notice: if you have children, it's easier to spot a passion in them at a young age. Kids express themselves more freely than adults do, so it's easier to see what they are interested in.

People have told me that I have a lot of hidden talents. They aren't really hidden, but rather they are dormant from non-use. You might have experienced this too. So, look for your dormant talents hiding right under the surface.

Take time to explore and give attention to them. You could develop new passions that you never knew you had! Now we have more clarity for the burning question!

HOW DO I FIND MY PASSION IN LIFE?

The good news is that the answer lies within us. Nobody can tell you what your passion is or what you are passionate about. You don't have to look further than yourself.

The only thing needed is you and your new passion recipe! I broke it down into the four parts so you can use it all the time, whenever you want!

I hope everybody can use this passion recipe to find all their passions and bring them out to share with the world. Imagine a world with everyone working on and pursuing their true passions in life. The happiness, joy and value creation would be endless! (**Please see next page for recipe!**)

PASSION RECIPE

- **ONE PART– You** and the person you want to become with your God-given gifts found and brought to the surface.

- **ONE PART– Gifts** turn into **talents** and skills that you hone for a specific purpose.

- **ONE PART– Love** is your enthusiastic motivation to use your talents and skills in service to others.

- **ONE PART– PASSION**! Newly found, creates amazing value for yourself and others, bringing: Wealth, Health, Peace, Joy, Happiness, Love…etc.

Chapter Five

SPIRITUALITY

SEEKING TRUTH

My thoughts on the topic of spirituality I would like to share with you have a lot to do with the concept of oneness, which is one of the things that I have been studying the most. I have been a truth seeker basically all my life, but it didn't really kick in until I started looking within myself instead of outside. At the time of this writing (2016), I am forty-two and I didn't start on the spiritual path until about 2009, when I was about thirty-six.

I am spiritual, not religious. Now, that may sound like a label but it's a chosen way of life. I am sure people have asked you this as they have me: What is the difference between being spiritual and or being religious or following a religion? Can you have both, or be both, would be the next question…

The answer is **Yes**, you can do or believe in whatever you want, but why stop there? The impulse to look within oneself and seek the truth is to dive into the mystery – as in "I want to find out what my truth is and what resonates with me. I want to know who I am and why I'm here." That same urge to know the truth is present in every human being.

Now of course, you don't have to be a truth seeker. It's fine to say, "I believe in this or that." But I would hold that, at some point after the endless stories we have been told, and being surrounded with other people's opinions, we eventually have to ask ourselves the big question.

"What resonates with me more, spirituality or religion?" Is it enough for me to follow the teachings of a religion, or am I being called to another, deeper exploration to discover who I really am? If you are having thoughts like this right now or at any time, you are already on the path of seeking the truth and more importantly, your truth.

Discovering the Truth of anything, big or small, arises in a process of breaking things down to their **ESSENCE**!

FINDING THE ESSENCE

There are many methods we could use to come to know the Essence of an idea or a thing. An example is science, where we attempt to make sense of things using objective reasoning and constructing a truth based on what is seen, heard and touched.

Another method to discover what is true would be the process of elimination, where one categorizes things to conclude that we have this and that fact, so then we can cancel out the non-relevant or considered to be untrue material.

There is also the vetting-out process. Here, information is gathered from many different sources, selecting those with the most validity and relevance to the subject in an attempt to gain more understanding.

All of these methods can be useful, but are time consuming. The best approach that I have found - and you can use it for anything – is simply putting things in their proper context with the **TRUTH**.

In other words, if the truth and facts are in the proper order the picture will be clear and not misinterpreted. With the truth setting you free and the proper context, one will be on the road to knowing what is really going on! So, what is going on, you say? You have heard that religion is a belief-system that is pre-determined, and spirituality means going within. That is a good beginning point.

We want an even deeper meaning; we want to get to the root of the matter. The life-changing understanding we come to have is that there is only one Truth. It is the same for everyone. The truth isn't about separating things and people; we get beyond thinking and saying, "I am this religion or that" or "I am spiritual and believe this way or the other."

The root, the base or essence of everything is **WE ARE ALL ONE!** Since we are all one, we are all doing the same thing. From the beginning of human life on earth and the formation of the religions and spiritual paths, we have all been heading to the same place, just taking different roads and turns to get there. That place is the next level of existence for mankind, a higher consciousness that embodies oneness and unity.

For instance, at a basic level we have all gone through this in our lives with a job or other people telling us, "It's my way, or the highway." The highway represents the path of freedom, yet we are told that doing things the old way is the only right option or way to go about things. Sometimes our spirit or Soul wants to break free and explore new ways of doing things. As long as the end result brings more good into life, then what difference does it make how we get there?

This is the path of unity, or the path where we are all one. We all have the same goal, and our path is the journey to enlightenment, or heading back to God, the Source, the Great Central Sun or whatever you prefer to call it. All of us, everybody on the planet now and all who have been here are **beautiful precious light beings**! We are all God's children on a mission to explore and experience.

LIGHT MISSION

As energy/light beings incarnated in the physical plane of existence, we are on a mission to transcend duality. As we learn lessons and rise above our different/unique perspectives on life, we leave separation behind and become one united front for peace and love!

In doing this, we are raising our consciousness, which is Soul growth culminating in a higher vibration for us and the planet Earth. It all comes down to everybody just living and experiencing life while giving loving service to others. We don't have to get caught up in petty squabbling about "my way is better than your way," "my belief is better than yours," always focusing on right and wrong ways, positive and negative...etc.

In our journey through human consciousness, it would be true to say that we are all of the Spirit, or Spiritual Beings.

Our religion could be described as: We are all one seeking the Kingdom of Heaven, The Summerland or Nirvana! The religion claimed or spirituality practiced is just a path we take.

One thing that is really good for us to know is that it's not possible for us to fail. In all the Universe/Multiverse, there isn't any such thing as retrogression or moving backwards, only progression. Every experience, no matter how difficult or sad it may be, is part of our learning in order to expand ourselves. So, in putting spirituality in the proper context, The spirit wants the soul to move forward and higher! We want to grow beyond the "D" for duality and have the spiritual you in a higher reality! Why is this so important?

All of us light beings are on our way to a higher energy level, and the new energy will not support the old. The evil and subversion and corruption that has been going on, past and present, will not be able to cross over to the higher vibrations that are entering the Earth plane at this time in our history.

God's wrath isn't about punishment. There is no "God" ruling over us and judging us. There is only the invitation of our Higher Selves wishing to bring us from a lower plane to a higher one, through love. Dear reader and new friend: Are you starting to see and understand what is going on now? We must have a higher vision than the current one, as separation will not get us there!

SPIRITUAL VISION

Did you know that Jerusalem means **"City of Peace"**? That is very interesting, isn't it? Let us explore this a little more and I think you will find what I have realized is very interesting as well!

Notice, a **higher vision** is of **peace**, not sacrifice! If one is going to have spiritual peace, there can't be visons of damnation to God's precious souls. So, one doesn't need a Bible or prophecy, only common sense, to tell you that if we are fighting around Jerusalem, we have majorly distorted that vision and **"Ascension is Near!"**

This is why it has been said that we have missed the writing on the wall, for the message has been brought down from on high many times over.

The message lies in "**Reaping what is sown!**" The meaning is that it's time to: **Leave behind/come out from under evil veils and illusions that are clouding the lower physical vision, and get under the shelter of Mother and Father God's loving embrace and awaken your higher spiritual vision!**

This means we should expect that the cyclic nature of karma – actions and their consequences – will continue to unfold until the third dimension is cleared and karma is no longer needed. The evil seeds that have been sown and manifested through lower thought-forms will reap a **density death and will not be repeated because of lessons learned and human consciousness raised to a higher level**. With this, mankind can evolve in a lighter density on a higher plane.

You might have heard something about mankind's second death. This isn't about doom/gloom and the reaper taking you to hell!

It's about the death/transcendence of man's animal nature and the spirit ascending once again. This means that, together, as **The Spirit of Christ**, we are ascending through man's lower nature and raising/returning to **Christ consciousness or The Divine Mind of God!**

THE KEY TO YOUR TRUTH

Questions are the key! If you want to find your personal truth and what resonates with you, questions are always helpful. We don't want to waste a lot of time, blindly following what others have said. If you don't believe that way or it somehow isn't resonating. You have to discover your own truth. Some questions are: What really resonates with me? Do I believe that? Is what I'm hearing the truth, or just someone's opinion?

On the road to finding truth, it's our job to keep questioning everything and try to make the best decisions we can in the moment. Whether you are just starting out on a spiritual path, just getting into religion or you have been navigating through one or the other for a while, I say, **find the truth for you!**

The passion formula you now have will help you with this as you learn to use stimulation as a guide.

This means becoming tuned in so you recognize when you get "lit up" or "turned on" by something. You can feel when your interest gets piqued in terms of what you are involved in, observing or practicing/being taught. Is it interesting and exciting to you to the point you would want to do it in your free time?

For example, in exploring my spirituality I became very interested in metaphysics and I am always reading or watching something about it. You learn to tune in to your intuition, which is your personal guidance system and trust your gut feeling and instincts.

SOUL GROWTH

The goal of our spirituality is **Soul growth**, and many things can contribute to this. This is why it's referred to as "going within yourself to explore and find out who you really are." If you are starting to wonder what your path is and what you are doing here, or what your mission/purpose is… then you are on the cusp of **a spiritual awakening!**

Everybody has their different assignments, but the mission is the same. Ultimately it's all about **LOVE**, learning to be love, give love, self-love and on it goes. I think we can safely say that wherever you put your foot next is your perfect path. Keep learning and moving forward!

Now, the moment you have been waiting for!

WHAT CAN I DO FOR SELF/SPIRITUAL GROWTH?

Some great books and profound material to read for spiritual growth are:

The Ra Material/Law of One. (Carla Rueckert, Don Elkins, James McCarty, 1981). There are five books that cover a lot of different spiritual teachings that were presented through channeling in the 1980's. Please visit www.llresearch.org for more information.

The Convoluted Universe (Dolores Cannon, 2001). There are five books in this series also. These books deal with people bringing out information of a spiritual nature through regression therapy.

The Power of Now; also *A New Earth* (Eckhart Tolle, 1999 and 2005). These two books are great also, talking about transcending the ego and living in the now with a vision for where human consciousness is heading.

WHAT WEBSITES CAN I EXPLORE?

www.thegoldenlightchannel.com This site has a lot of spiritual messages and articles to read pertaining to ascension.

www.galacticconnection.com This site has daily alternative news on many different subjects and topics that deal with spirituality and our galactic nature with many things to explore through videos, radio shows, articles...etc.

RIDDLE...

I am comprised of only four letters, but my word and meaning knows no bounds.

I am the strongest energy, and no vibration in the whole multiverse equals my sound.

I come straight from the Source, from the All that Is and sprinkle down on you like a shower.

Your heart harnesses the emotion of me, and I am the essence of a flower.

In your head, I transmit my thought. I am extremely complex and hard to be taught.

I am light and come as a gift. If you are open to receive me, there will be a shift!

WHAT AM I?

Chapter Six

LOVE

GETTING TO KNOW LOVE

If God is the essence of love and love is in all things, then what is love? That sounds pretty deep, right? The answer is actually very simple. **LOVE** is: Humor, joy, bliss, abundance, fun, gratitude, beauty, light-filled, play-full, opulence, nature and all of us!

God is love, we are God and God is us! You can find love in all things and as individuals we can experience it in a lot of different ways that are very meaningful to us or resonate deeply within our being.

For example, some people can just watch animals in nature and start crying - that would be them feeling love for animals. How about beautiful orchestrated music, like music of the angels? The sound vibration will touch your soul and has the power to change your **DNA** – that is love!

We will talk about that more later in the chapter. For now, the way love expresses itself through nature is very interesting!

CHANGING POWER

I think it's safe to say that the power of love brings on massive change! For instance, the caterpillar transforming into a butterfly, that is a big change! The caterpillar represents the old way that is getting there with legs, slowly like traveling through something heavy and dense.

The cocoon is the love energy/catalyst that morphs it into something beautiful, very light and it can then fly with wings/speed. The butterfly is evidence of major change through loving energy that is visible and felt through beauty and Grace.

Have you noticed in these times of **major change**, we are starting to see more butterflies around? This is because our vibrations are rising and so is the vibration of the planet.

As we evolve, the compassion and love growth is related to our maturity. Through my inner exploration and research into the nature of life, I have come to understand that our souls at one time or another have to experience everything in life for growth, such as: A rock, tree, elemental energy and animals…etc. The next step, when ready, is becoming a complex human. The idea is that we are learning love through different forms. Once we have mastered the experience, the time comes to move on.

ASPECTS OF LOVE

Love is in everything. We are constantly observing and learning from it. Some aspects are: Romantic love, love for family, children, friends, pets, your favorite creations in life, and life in general.

How about your love for reading, learning and books? Love is supposed to be fun! I hope you are having a good time and enjoying yourself and the book so far, right now!

Is it possible to get your **laugh** on and your **learn** on at the same time? **"Indeed it is!" Show Me The Love!** If someone is showing you the love and you are laughing/joyful, then your vibration gets higher and you will be feeling great!

LOVE INTERMISSION

This chapter completes the first section of the book and of course, I wanted the love chapter to be fun and light-filled! In section two, we will be switching gears a little bit and moving on to other interesting topics and subjects. If you are still reading now, you must be interested, stimulated and enjoying yourself, which is what we want!

So, kick back in your favorite chair, take a break, have a drink and maybe some good eats! If the first section wasn't mind expanding enough, don't worry, I have more crazy news for you or **"Kray, Kray"** with a capital **K**, if you prefer!

Some would also say, it's bordering on **"Awesome Sauce!"** I like that little saying, it's pretty funny! This would be love coming through humor! It puts a smile on your face and gives you the giggles, you know, like what you're doing right now!

It reminds me of cooking. I like to fix up some premium eats **(Organic of course)** and I think I'm getting pretty good at it! I have some good recipes, like my own version of chicken spaghetti – everybody loves that! I am learning to cook more vegan food now, also.

You know how people say they put a lot of **love** into their cooking? Well, that is exactly what's happening! You can put your energy into your food while cooking or right before you eat and it lasts about three hours or so.

All you do is focus on your food and put your loving energy into it with the conscious intention of it being **pure, nutritious, life giving** and of course, **delicious!**

Cooking is good in general. It's good creative action for you and your spouse or friends getting together. Cooking can be especially good if you like a little wine with your meal or getting your cook on with a little Vino also. Then it is the same as cooking good with the **sauce** and **on the sauce!**

Are you getting hungry now? If we have more people doing these things, we will reach the next evolution of love, very fast!

Now, let's check out some questions for **love**!

WHAT CAN I DO FOR MORE LOVE?

www.theearthdiet.com On this site you will find the *Earth Diet Book*. It has many healthy, organic recipes for all kinds of different food with fitness, great health and love in mind. There is other content here as well, such as articles about healthy living and a radio show. This site is all about spreading the love and knowledge around to help people.

WHAT CAN I LISTEN TO?

www.shekinaspeaks.com   This site has the music of the angels and other orchestrated material with videos to enjoy.

www.crystalmagicorchestra.com. Both of these sites deal with music in the **528 hertz range.** This is the love frequency or language of light that is geared towards **DNA** activation. There is also a lot of material to read and listen to.

WHAT CAN I READ?

Super Puzzle (Mark Hamilton, 2012). This is the best book I have found on love. I highly recommend it! It also does a good job with taking you into the next evolution of love. There are three books navigating a story of twelve kids who grow up to be super achievers, talking about the love that got them there and then using/giving back that love to the wonderful blue planet.

SECTION TWO

MANIFEST YOUR DESTINY

Chapter Seven

TRUTH

EXPLORING TRUTH

"What do you know, What do you hear? What do you say?" This famous little line, usually found in mob movies, is relevant to what goes on in the world concerning the truth. It translates to: We know a lot and we hear a good bit, but we only share a little. Why? Because of course, **YOU Can't Handle The Truth!** The answer to that funny but arrogant statement would be: "How would you know, I need to get some first!"

The truth should be served up like a premium organic dinner, where we would say: "I like that, let me have some please, and keep it coming!" We touched on the truth in the spirituality chapter, but now it's time to really explore it in detail and find out how important the truth really is for everybody!

Did you know that **YES** is the only positive response to anything we face in life? If you are saying yes to life then you are taking the good and the bad together, moving forward in a positive fashion, hopefully with the truth of the matter at hand. On the other hand, No would be responding negatively like you have to defend yourself or conceal a situation. Hence, "No I will not tell you the truth!" My point as it relates to this discussion/topic is, in regards to us as humans not settling for anything but a positive outcome and doing our best to manifest it. This relates to dealing with life as it comes and as the Champion that you are! I learned that from Dr. Coldwell, among many other things. I think the word **TRUTH** is a very important quality to have in our arsenal. There are many different attributes of truth, such as: Trusting in ourselves/others and being Trustworthy; Having a high personal integrity; and associating with those who also operate from high integrity; Being Honest and keeping your word. All of these aspects or expressions have one thing in common, and that is, they all deal with actions of being true within oneself and positive.

The opposite of this is obviously falsehood and that brings negative consequences such as deceiving and misleading oneself and others, lying, cheating, and stealing. These are the acts of not being in alignment with one's True Nature. Such actions reflect a psychological state in which a person has come to believe that he or she has to subjugate and use others in order to gain advantage, or in order to survive. This is classic victim consciousness that Earth inhabitants need to conquer. This belief leads to justification of misrepresentation for the purpose of pulling the wool over another one's eyes and, in even darker scenarios, recruiting someone to follow the wrong/dark path.

The truth is of the Light, emanating from a Higher Frequency and inviting us to remember where we originally came from. Seeking to live in the vibration of Truth and of Light will lead us down the proper path and all the way back to the source/God! Why would anyone want to hide the truth and have the intention of misleading someone on purpose? The answer is, for power and unearned advantages or to gain control over the ill-informed or people deemed lesser than/unequal to others in one's group or family.

As you know, this pattern of collusion and corruption has been going on for eons and is still a major annoyance to deal with today. There are countless examples we could offer of this type of behavior which all of us have experienced, but we want to keep the focus on recognizing lies and deception when it makes an appearance. In doing so, we can choose to transcend these experiences and allow only what is True to grow in our lives.

NURTURING TRUTH

It has been said that Trust is like an orchid flower, beautiful and bright, but very delicate. If it doesn't get the proper nourishing it will die. Trust is the first thing that takes a hit in any type of relationship and is incredibly hard to gain back once it is lost. If truth isn't part of one's resolve, then there isn't any way to be trustworthy. So, if there is deception built into the first impression, it could be very hard to redeem oneself.

We have all heard that "the truth hurts!" The truth is supposed to be good – why would it hurt? Coming from a personal growth standpoint, the truth hurts sometimes because we are holding a false idea of ourselves/ reality and the truth comes to us from a higher source – or someone we love! – to give us a wake-up call and get us back on track. The answers are right there within the questioning of it. If you feel that something is off, doesn't make sense, isn't resonating with you, you're getting bad vibes, **(Negative Vibrations)** or your instincts are saying: **"Run Away!"** then something is wrong!

We need to pay attention (**be Awake**) because the best lies are carefully constructed to contain some truth, but have their **roots** in deception. This is the basic formula for "hiding out in the open." You have seen this countless times in the form of beguiling ads or letters, carefully crafted by deceitful people, assorted abusers and dark ones that carry the purpose of keeping us entrapped and asleep. Probably one of the most prevalent forms of mind control is **symbolism**! The dollar bill is a good example of this. You can find the esoteric knowledge concerning the image of the eye in the pyramid that appears on our currency, if you are interested.

So, why should the truth hurt? Ordinarily, you are given only a little bit so you will stay satisfied and not think too deeply. It can't be too much, or you will figure out the real truth and you will wake up and have to face some pain. Why? Because you realize you have been deceived, lied to, hoodwinked, duped, and gotten over on. It is imperative that we as an advancing society not only recognize but stop the intentional deceiving of each other like that is perfectly okay, as a people we must embrace the truth on all fronts and keep learning how to deal with it properly!

There is a book you can check out called **Who Needs Light** that explains this type of deception and talks about root causes/identifying people or abusers with ill intent who are trying to deceive you in some way.

When you are in touch with the truth, the vibrational flow is good, you feel fine, things resonate with you properly and leave you with positive vibes or **good vibrations!** You understand things easily without worries or doubts, and everything makes sense. You naturally know how to respond in a situation or the next step to take.

So, now that you are reading this and thinking about it, would you consider yourself a **truth seeker?** I think everybody naturally has a little bit of a truth seeker in them. The kicker is, truth and honesty is our birthright and we shouldn't have to seek it! Unfortunately for us, at this time, Truth is something we need to awaken to and consciously choose.

Another name for a truth seeker is **Rainbow Warrior.** Such a person has the traits of: Trustworthiness, a sense of faith/knowingness, honesty, genuineness/authenticity, high morality/ethics and a commitment to becoming free. For more information on this please see:

www.fractalenlightenment.com

TRUTH SEEKING

We were talking about symbolism earlier and how it relates to things. The deck of playing cards is actually an interesting tool that can be utilized for the purpose of recognizing deception. You can think of it as a template to start from on a smaller scale that will help you recognize deceit on a larger one. If someone is going to become a master poker player, for example, the level of deception that is needed would be unknown to the beginner. Until he also, learns and adapts to the art of it. The "art of deception" is just like the "art of war" as in, there is a specific method to the madness. People with bad intentions have been practicing and perfecting these negative skills for a very long time. It is up to us to explore and seek the truth, honing are own skills in the "art of truth and empowerment."

This all has to due with suppressing human consciousness and advancement as we will continue to talk about in this chapter. If you are familiar with the Tarot card deck and the twenty-one Major Arcana, it is the same way but even more important. Aspects of it were suppressed so it couldn't be used so easily as a tool to learn about the Divine and awaken higher consciousness. As you can see with these card examples, (above and next) we get a little and we have to do our due diligence to find out more.

There is a very special book that goes into detail about this. The author has actually used cards and poker to develop new technologies and presents information on how to recognize deception on a massive scale. We will note this with the questions on what to read.

So, with a deck of cards, the ace of spades is the big significant one. It's like an emblem or symbol for secrets and is proclaimed to be a key to mysteries. It represents the truth that lies behind **veils of illusion**. I am all about calling the spade a spade, as in seeing past illusions and finding the real truth. It also represents change and transformation, which is exactly what happens as soon as the truth comes out or is exposed!

TRUTH SUPPRESSION

One of the biggest challenges that the whole world has had to endure since the beginning of days, is: **Suppression of the Truth**! This includes all kinds of knowledge, creations/inventions and people with new and great ideas from a macro level to a micro level. Also, I'm sure there's a ton of things we don't have any knowledge about because so much has been hidden from us. Obviously, there are plenty of examples to discover, but we will mention a few to get the gist of it.

The suppression of patents on inventions is a huge one! Thousands of patents have been withheld, including: Free energy devices, propulsion systems, holistic health technologies and basically anything that threatens the use of fossil fuels, with oil being the number one monopoly that is poised to fall. Free energy technology threatens the power, control and money empire that has reigned over the earth.

Consider Nikola Tesla for example: he had all kinds of inventions and ideas for free energy that never saw the light of day. Why? We should have given a person with his genius all the resources and assistance possible!

The suppression of people and their wonderful life/planet evolving ideas has been going on for far too long, by a small group attempting to maintain power and control over others. This cannot continue with a planet transitioning into a higher dimension!

Contrary to popular belief/opinion, oil isn't liquid gold! It's **Mother Earth's** life/blood equivalent. Fracking is basically stealing blood from mother earth! This contaminates the water, causing a negative energy effect. This is one of the reasons for earthquakes! Gaia responds in kind trying to shake it off, so to speak and clear that energy.

The Earth is a living organism, similar to an animal in a way. Animals are very good at taking negative energy from humans and transmuting it, but not if they are sick or have a poor diet. The earth is hurting from all of these negative energies, and the drastic weather changes reflect this. If it's raining heavily, this is mother Earth's way of cleansing the air. This is why it's called **Liquid Sunshine!** The rain is nourishing us and cleansing the planet, just like the sun does!

What is needed is to have the free energy technology available to everyone and start using it ASAP! WE need to clean up the planet and get off the dependency to fossil fuels which is draining the earth dry!

Another big area of suppression is health technologies, as in holistic and alternative ways of treatment. Everybody knows the main suppression reason for this, which is money. Some people think that there is no money in the cure, like it is okay to continue to capitalize off of the sick. Of course, the pharmaceutical and health industries would take a massive hit if all the good people became aware of and started taking advantage of newly available and released technologies, that could treat big diseases like cancer in a less costly manner and highly effective ways. As you have probably figured out by now, chemotherapy and drugs just make people sicker and may contribute to early and unnecessary death, usurping wealth along the way.

I want to encourage everybody who reads this to explore alternative treatment options for taking care of your health.

With the information in this book and your own research, you will be able to find plenty of alternative means to take good care of yourself, loved ones, family and friends!

Another thing that has been held back is knowledge of our spiritual freedom. We are spiritual energy beings, which means we are **very powerful souls!** The bad news is we have been held back through disinformation and suppression of our true nature. The good news is, we cannot be stopped or held back any longer! Now, this brings up some questions of why and how? We know the why, which is all about suppressing the populace and keeping us in the dark, so we can't rise up and challenge the so-called "powers that were." The question is, how does a situation like this manage to come about?

It starts with paradigms that include many bad habits. These habits grow wild in people and they basically become **power mad!** The result is fear, greed, focusing on lack instead of abundance and every other negative thing in the dark play list which has been passed on from generation to generation. Now, I'm sure you can imagine the snowball effect, with everything in between leading up to now and what we see today. This is what forms the pyramid of so-called authority and power.

The edifice of power is built with only fear and lies holding it together, suppressing every truth that is available on myriad levels of our reality. More illusions form under a cloak of lies, resulting in a hierarchy with each level not knowing as much as the last/next. This infrastructure has endured due to lack of trust in anyone or anything after generations of enslavement and rough treatment, as happens on the dark path. This type of fraudulent foundation without the light and truth will crumble under its own weight.

Negative/dark energy is heavy, and positive energy is light. Guess how much your soul weighs? Only about **Twenty-One Grams**! The heavy/dark energy can't hold our light-filled/light-as-a-feather soul. It will eventually break out of there, just like we are doing now!!

Now for the interesting part! Why would a **pyramid of illusions** come complete with a bright and shiny cherry on top, or shall we say, illuminated golden eye candy? Remember symbolism? If you break out a dollar bill right now, you will know exactly what I am talking about. This brings up many questions, such as: If the path to God is through illumination, why is it so hard to get there? Why are there so many lies? What's going on? You see, these questions popping up again don't make any sense until we put them in the proper context of the truth.

It's hard to get there because people don't have the truth! **What is the Truth?** Let's break it down with our new knowledge together, shall we?

The **pyramid** represents the dishonest part. Let's call it the hierarchy of tyrant falsehood. The **eye** is a **symbol** cloaked in multiple meanings, with the truth part in there somewhere. So, it's out in the open, but hiding! Here is your little bit, but not too much. Otherwise, you will see the devious plan cloaked under a thick **veil of illusions**. If that happens, you would be hurt and uncontrollable, which would lead to the crumbling of the would-be tyrannical plan. We do not need to be in revolt all the time, the key is awareness and not continuing down the same dark path.

So, it's our job to ask the hard questions and sift through all the lies and find the **Golden Truth!** Conveniently, the **eye** represents the **pineal gland** that everybody has also called the **third eye**. This just happens to be your own personal **star gate** and access to the **spirit world!** Suppression of this access was perpetrated on humanity in order to maintain control.

THE TRUTH OF THE PINEAL GLAND

Your pineal gland does much more than regulate your sleep patterns when it's time to go night, night! Have you ever heard the expression, **"I live beyond the gate?"** The meaning is that we are more than flesh, blood and bones.

We all are star/light-energy beings who live beyond the gate, or physical realm, and the pineal gland is our access point!

So, put in the proper context here and armed with the truth, you can see how somebody wanting to control and enslave others with a negative agenda wouldn't want the populace to know or have this information.

Have you ever seen pictures or statues of a pine cone appearing in various places in religious art or even on your own porch at home? This a representation of the pineal gland, which is only about the size of a pea in the center of your head and resembles a pine cone figure. The pineal gland can become hardened and/or calcified and then, of course, it doesn't work very well. If this happens, a person's physic abilities are greatly reduced along with their connection to the Source.

The main things to stay away from, that cause calcification are: Fluoride, mercury and chlorine among other toxic chemicals. Fluoride is found in tooth paste, water, vaccines…etc. Mercury is in new light bulbs, maybe old cavity fillings, technology devices…etc. Chlorine is in pools and chemical products…etc.

The pineal gland puts out dimethyltryptamine, or **DMT** for short, which is known as the "spirit molecule" because it helps you connect with the spirit world. Also, the pineal gland secretes your own natural version of **HGH** or Human Growth Hormone which helps the body heal itself naturally. So, I'm sure you can see why it's so important!

We, the people, need to be illuminated with the truth! We will then awaken to the real world and see that the pyramid and everything it stands for serves the purpose of enlightening us to a new reality!

MORE TRUTH TO COME

All of this material that we have been talking about deals with total **truth disclosure**. This is finally coming as the **matrix of illusions** crumbles. Just like what is happening in this moment, the real truth will continue to reveal itself through multiple channels as we go forward.

Now for some resources to help find the truth! I have a few things for you to check out, and then I am going to give you my truth seeking technique. You can put it to good use and start searching for your own truths if you want. Please, look at these subjects we are and will be talking about or anything else you are interested in. Good luck and have fun seeking the **truth**! (Please turn the next page!)

WHAT CAN I DO FOR TRUTH SEEKING?

www.3rdeyeactivation.com For good articles and information on the pineal gland.

www.GoodGopher.com   This is an alternative search engine for truth seekers that filters out disinformation.

WHAT CAN I READ FOR THE TRUTH?

Dishonest Money: Financing the Road to Ruin (Joseph Plummer, 2008). This book tracks the origins of money up through time to the present, talking about money and the banking system.

Poker: A Guaranteed Income for Life Using the Advanced Concepts of Poker (Frank R. Wallace, 1972). The other book that goes along with this is **Roots**. (Frank R. Wallace, 1981). These two books deal with learning how to recognize deception through the art of poker playing. They also talk about how to apply the concepts to improve everyday life and live in truth.

TRUTH SEEKING TECHNIQUE

- 1 – Associate yourself with honest, genuine, and ethical people you can trust who have a like mind.

- 2 – Branch off to explore recommended people, books, audios and material of all kinds that you are drawn to.

- 3 – Do your own vetting of found information, people, opinions, ideas and philosophies.

- 4 – If things are resonating with you, i.e., they feel good, sound great, are enjoyable, truthful and have Rainbow Warrior qualities… then make it your truth until proven otherwise. Go from there with an open mind and repeat process.

Chapter Eight

SUCCESS

The power for success lies within your own magnetic spirit.
Attract that which you feel and imagine for life, through mind,
heart and soul. Realize your desires through dreams and belief.

First, I would like you to know that you are already successful! Everybody deserves success through wealth, health, peace, freedom and abundance. It all comes down to your self-worth, self-love and self-respect. Know that you are already a **Champion and Somebody!**

So, what is the key to success? How do you achieve success? What are the steps to success? Are you tired of the age-old questions? Guess what? I have a refreshing concept for you! I am here to inform you that it has nothing to do with money!!

Are you surprised? OMG!! What? So, what's it all about, you say? What's the HAP'S! "The good gossip!" "Crack-a-lack-n!" And The "Deal of the O?" Or shall we say, the politically correct version? What's the progressively stimulating jargon of a new idea or philosophy? Okay, I won't keep everybody in suspense… It is **YOU**! The only thing you need for success is yourself! Who you are is your success, not what you have in the way of material things or accomplishments.

YOU ARE THE DREAM

It has been said that "Success is the progressive realization of a worth-while dream." I believe this to be true, but on a basic level. If you consider yourself a dreamer and the ideas or thoughts you have become reality, then the success that comes from it is definitely worth it. Nothing happens without you, that makes you the dream! The realization is that there is no success without you "dreaming" in the first place! The whole concept of "The Dream" and variations of thought progression is very interesting and let us say, fully involved! When in the sleep state, we are at a very high awareness and closer to the Source Field where we can access that energy through dreams. In this state, we are creating whatever we want with our thoughts freely and manifesting things faster or even instantly. This is our true nature, the hard part is bringing this easy and grace through to our third dimensional reality.

Now, when we wake up and we're in a conscious state, the whole act of physicality is an illusion. Why? It is an illusion because we need an avatar (your body) to move about and experience the physical realm and our thoughts, dreams and ideas have to go through a third dimensional time delay. Not to mention, deal with the conscious mind and ego. Guess what ego means: Edging God Out! This means that our whole waking consciousness is a dream. In other words, as God creates through us, we give reality a place to be recognized. So, what does this mean?

We can rephrase the little saying so it's better suited for all:

"Success is being the conduit within one's field of influence, magnetizing positive thoughts to himself/herself with noteworthy dreams, which create God miracles everyday."

On that note, a rule of thumb would be: Always act on your highest excitement and/or highest imagining, which brings positive creation.

SUCCESS TRAINING

We all find ourselves here together at the **Earth School**, and this is considered to be the proving grounds. It doesn't matter if you have been here only a few hours, thirty, fifty or a hundred years. Only the bravest souls come here! This makes you successful from the start!

The last thing the good people need is a society that has become consumed by greed, telling them to gauge their self-worth by made-up debt currency in an illusionary realm. It is true: life is a game and while we are here, we want to set ourselves up to win. How do we win? The way to win is knowing the rules and the score.

The Rules are what you decide and make them out to be, as in: **Nobody tells you what to do!** Believe in yourself first and foremost; also know that you are doing the right things. The Score is always in your favor and you win through **self-mastery!** You never stop learning and integrating new knowledge into your positive, created reality.

The training for success reflects all possibilities through lessons to be learned. This often starts at a very dense form of expression and continues upward. The little to big, countless challenges coming to us are masked as future problems. The thing to know is that there aren't any problems. Only situations, opportunities and challenges from which we learn and grow.

We as humans have been masters at creating problems where none exist. This is encouraged through the implementation of policies or rules/regulations that put ourselves and everybody else under hindered conditions. Basically, we are programmed to put major limits on ourselves when we are actually limitless beings.

This can also be thought of as the act of self-sabotage, and that isn't good for anybody. I personally have had a lot of experience with this, and it is hard to overcome!

LEARNING SELF-LOVE

Whatever you want to do in life, the important thing is **Self-Love!!** You definitely want to surround yourself with all things positive, drama-free and stress-free as much as possible. Have you heard the expression: "Your income will be the average of your five best friend's?"

Why is this so, and is it good or bad? Good/positive friends uplift, support/ encourage you and embody qualities of success themselves that you can emulate. Such friends are loyal to you, care for/love you and are optimistic. Bad/negative friends envy you and hate your success because it makes them take a look at themselves and then they see failure. They are pessimistic and want you to remain on a loser level with them, so they will feel better about themselves. They degrade and keep you down, and as Dr. Coldwell says, they are cancer seeds and you have to cut them out of your life!

Once your vibration increases and changes, your positive relationships will get better and stronger. The negative ones will fall away and you will be left with friendships/relationships with like-minded, positive people who are committed to the path of success, like you.

It is also good to stir things up in your life, such as: Get out of your normal routines, go to new places or on vacation. These things expand your con- sciousness and help you clarify what really matters to you on a personal level. Also, stirring things up gets you looking at things with fresh eyes and, of course, have fun while you're at it!

SUCCESS CONDITIONING

A very important tool for success is **Reading!** Everything we are talking about here in this book involves reading to further your knowledge. Like we have been talking about, you want the best and most profound material you can get. Why? Because leaders are always readers! It is good to be constantly reading and educating yourself on the things that interest you in one way or another.

Reading, attending seminars/workshops, becoming an apprentice/finding a mentor, listening to audio/video talks and teachings all contribute in positive ways. This is lifelong conditioning for your success that you never stop. So, it's good to be open to new ideas and ways of thinking.

SUCCESSFUL TRAITS

If you want to be a self-leader, then your strength is **Self-Sufficiency.** On the other end, weakness is following others blindly and perpetuating their goals/dreams instead of your own. It is obviously never good to follow someone who is already following someone else down the wrong path.

I'm sure that you have heard and read many things that talk about charac-
ter traits for success, such as: Persistence, being relentless, perseverance,
mental strength and high focus to get things done. We will be talking about
some books in a minute that relate to this kind of thing.

Now, you might be thinking to yourself, why does it have to be so hard,
and why do I have to have these traits in order to succeed? The answer is
Chaos! The action of creating something, your desires, goals and dreams
are in the chaos stage while you are forming your creation. Within this
chaos stage there is a lot happening. On one hand we have to deal with
Entropy, a force where things are constantly being pulled apart bringing
about disorder. And on the other, divine timing also comes into play. If
the timing is not right for some reason, then there will be delays of some
sort. This is why it is so crazy trying to achieve your goals and why it is
so important to utilize positive success traits!

You, the person, are already the embodiment of success! You use the
gift of yourself and these traits as tools to get the job done and manifest
your creations.

You might have also heard, **"Success is a decision away!"** This is true,
but I think a better statement would be: **"I am a successful creator and
my new creation is a decision away!"** This comes when you decide
to put your foot down and say: **I am done wishing it and dreaming**

it, I am doing it!! Then you use your tools and have a rage to succeed or a sense of urgency to get your creation to fruition with an energy wave of multiple thoughts and ideas.

In concluding our talk about success, please remember that true success at its core is **value creation** for the world, in service to others. The human destiny is to create; you came here as a Master Creator and already embody success. The idea is to keep moving forward, as you are never done and there isn't any set destination, with self-mastery being the ultimate goal on this journey. Please don't settle or make compromises with yourself. You never want to be comfortable with mediocrity and you can always contribute to changing the world by becoming the best version you can possibly be of your True Self.

We talked about reading being a necessary thing to do, so I have some great material for you and then I am going to give you a success design to help you with your creations. Whatever you are trying to create, look for the best materials possible relating to your ideas and thoughts. Begin with reading first, then workshops and audio… etc. After you have your dream clearly defined or your **chief aim**, you can use your new tools to create whatever your heart desires! **(Please see next page!)**

WHAT IS GOOD TO READ FOR SUCCESS?

Think and Grow Rich (Napoleon Hill, 2015) and another one by the same author is ***Law of Success in Sixteen Lessons***. Both of these books cover some of the traits we talked about and are very good for success training and knowledge.

The Magic of Believing (Claude M. Bristol, 1991). This book talks about how strong belief is and how to utilize it for your life.

The Only Answer to Success: You Were Born to be a Champion (Dr. Leonard Coldwell, 2010). This book talks about multiple techniques for bringing out the champion in you, for great success. Check out:

www.instinctbasedmedicinestore.com to find it.

WHAT WEBSITE CAN I LOOK AT?

www.selfgrowth.com   On this site you can find all kinds of material for self-improvement.

MY CHAMPION SUCCESS DESIGN

- 1 – I am the embodiment of a successful **champion**, starting out as a master creator!

- 2 – I know that success and my creation will come to fruition when I make a decision and commit to it 100%!

- 3 – I use my tools of persistence, perseverance and relentlessness to combat and overcome the **chaos** in designing my new ideas, inventions and creations!

- 4 – I have a rage to **succeed!** My determination knows no end, I trust/believe in myself, skills and abilities. I know my creation will **manifest** as I ride this powerful **Source energy wave that I have attracted to my reality!**

Matrix construct, an illusionary idol
Consuming Mother Earth's resources and rye.
Causing man's downfall
And the populace to die.

A service to self agenda
Intent on ruling land and sky.
For the wise believe in unity
And take no pleasure in the
Corrupt invasion of the dual reality.
Faulty Drone, am I?

Unearned glory gained,
Equals inequality for us.
Survival of the fittest, a must?

Who is this fake person called; Minority,
Strawman and Faulty Drone?
Labeled by a known, criminal empire
Falling off a paper throne.

Blind to see that only a higher vibration
Will advance to the next dimension.
Ascending through a frequency sick home.

Why drain the precious morsel dry?
Like an energy vampire clone, who doesn't cry.
Soulless in a God given skin,
Fully aware that time is running thin.

Emotionless and power mad,
Who is at fault in the cracked mirror?
If greed rules the day,
Holding all the gold stone won't make it clear!

Truth be told! The Light Alliance
And the New Golden Age is here!
This Faulty Drone spoken of,
Does he get one percent of the pie?

Behold! We all have our
Ninety-nine crosses to bear.
Thank Mother and Father God
We are awake and aware!

Surely it is not I!
For we, the wise and free
Will inherit an equal share.

Chapter Nine

FREEDOM

WHAT'S IT GOING TO TAKE?

Are we truly free? What constitutes freedom? Peace, liberty, justice and being able to go where you want to go and do what you want to do without restrictions, is nice. The only thing is, these things can be taken away, messed with and interrupted. Our freedoms have gotten really contorted since the original plan of our forefathers.

We should not have to fight for the freedom of speech, press/religion or anything else a free society wants to do. War and fighting is not the answer for anything, period and I think we have proved it by now! Fighting for freedom doesn't have to be violent with threats of weapons. We do although, have to have a united front for peace, positive solutions to long standing issues and leaders who have the pure intent to see it through. Especially if we are going to acquire it on a global level.

I was just thinking the same thing you were: Why is it so hard to have peace? People/humans, as you know, are complex. It has a lot to do with cultivating a belief in oneself, discovering self-love, self-esteem and self-empowerment.

Have you ever given somebody a compliment, telling them they are beautiful or an amazing person and noticed a weird reaction? If they have a good self-image and are pretty positive, they will light up like an angel! If not, you get a weird look, like what do you want from me? They act as if they can't believe somebody is being nice to them. This is because many people have a hard time experiencing positive energy. They may just choose not to know that experience, but either way, you can bet they are in great pain.

So, for peace to reign on planet Earth, all people need to believe it is possible in the first place. We need to have not only self-love but **LOVE** for everything and everyone, (**All Life and Planet!**) The big question is, what's it going to take to get there? We could take many different directions on the road to freedom, but I think the key focus for freedom and peace should be: **Self-Empowerment and knowing our Self-Worth!**

PROTESTING MOTHERS

Have you noticed that when something is wrong, like a tornado is coming, we see animals all of a sudden running the other way? They can sense that something bad is coming. This has a direct correlation to a mother's intuition. When we see so many mothers protesting in the streets, something must be very wrong!

When we see a **mother,** our **Mother** and **Mother Earth** in a state of destitution, impoverished and in need of aid, this is a calling that requires massive and immediate attention/action and must be responded to! This is the very definition of necessitousness, that has been talked about so many times before, to no avail. We can't avoid the **call** any longer!

Therefore, mankind, as in sons and daughters of God, is not **FREE** in a necessitous state. The good news is, this is where **NESARA** comes in – true freedom! We will talk about this in more detail later in the chapter.

For true freedom, we need the tools for empowerment and to raise/realize our true self-worth. Everything we are talking about in this book deals with your empowerment in some way that leads to you being as free as possible, and in control of your own destiny. We do this by adapting a new focus on freedom and shifting our consciousness to self-empowerment and self-growth. This will help us with realizing our true/full self-worth also.

Now, in order to do that and understand this, we need to talk about something everybody does every-day. We've had the freedom to chase the "American Dream," but never imagined we would have to **work** so hard to get it!

LOSING OUR WAY

In our short time here on earth, we have come a long way just to be about three thousand years behind. Everything we have done and will do comes from us being master creators of valuable knowledge for humanity. The relevant knowledge inspiring powerful thoughts and ideas for new creations, come from a free spirit.

What happens when you stifle a free spirit? He/she stops creating the new and continues producing the old. Competition sets in and we begin fighting to maintain an old system. This is why we have to be moving forward and growing or we will be moving backward and dying. At this crossroads, the only thing that plunges us forward is an open mind with courage/desire and a willingness to live in the unknown.

What is it going to take to propel us earthlings further? We have to remember that fear will only hold us back and love is the all-powerful energy for massive change.

We have been reduced down to something we are not, to a level that has been created/reached by our own doing. I'm sure **God** never intended for us to end up like we have. This state we are in is a by-product of separation and disconnection from the source. **WHO ARE WE?** First, let's talk about **WHO WE ARE NOT!**

WHO WE ARE NOT

We are not **Minorities!** When we label ourselves or others this way, it means someone who is lesser than/half of the whole, or considered not equal to. I am willing to bet that **Mother and Father God** take a breath and bow their heads every time they hear this, as this is the antithesis of our truth, which is unity with Christ consciousness!

There isn't any such thing as a minority, only an individual's contorted perspective of another being, human or otherwise. Some person is viewing another person in a holier-than-thou fashion and of lesser value because of their skin color or station in life.

All Light Beings, through their soul contracts at one time or another, past life or present, have played the role of a viewed-upon and so-called minority. It doesn't make a person better than anybody else because they have a certain color or higher station now, in this third dimensional lifetime!

We are not **numbers, labels and colors! We are not** so-called **FICA scores** made up out of thin air with an algorithm. Our names have meaning, and we are not even talking about our individual soul names. This is the same for employee numbers, blue shirts, or any other color that corresponds with some brand name or business.

An individual can't expect to rise up higher by tearing down another of God's precious souls. This is the kind of mentality that keeps all of us down and unable to press forward. The Truth is that we are all like entrepreneurs going about our lives trying to create value for our fellow man and progressing civilization to new heights of advancement.

WORK CHANNELS

All of these things that we do, whether it is a collective effort or an individual one, are just channels of God (or Soul or Self) expression. The ultimate source for a job, business or income, comes from the Universe. This is because we get everything we need from the Source/Ether. Overcoming competitive squandering of resources we shouldn't be using in the first place comes from understanding this and getting rid of lack and limitation.

It might be we have gotten into a position where we are working really hard and spending a lot of time doing things we don't necessarily want to be doing, repeating the same thing say-in, day-out. In this mode, we perform forty, sixty or more hours a week just to have the basics of survival in food, clothing and shelter. It is easy to fall into a perpetual, stagnant rut where we can't move forward. I consider this type of **W.O.R.K to be: Wasting Our Relevant Knowledge!!**

So, if the dead-end tasks that we find ourselves doing/performing inhibit soul growth and stifle our passion in life for what is truly important to us, then this only perpetuates the old burned-out paradigm.

The new comes from us using our relevant knowledge acquired when we are acting on our highest excitement and pursuing passions in life on a vector of joy/creation. This would be a true **free spirit/people!**

We would not be able to advance as a civilization, free or otherwise, if the focus were to remain on the negative and the past. The act of trying to control or fix things only makes it worse. When this is the main focus we end up creating more negativity and stagnation. This is the mode of living we were handed at birth, continually bombarded with the so-called "war" on everything, that perpetuates fear.

Remember when we were talking about negative goal-setting brought about by worrying and fear? If we are not focusing our vibrations on positive things like peace/love and creativity/unity, then we are using our imaginations to miscreate. In turn, this leads to creating hell on earth!

If you are doing a job that you love and your work brings you expansion, learning, and a sense of personal fulfillment, you are not wasting your time or relevant knowledge by working. Your job at that point is love. You are planting seeds and spreading your love/essence around. When this occurs, it isn't a burden anymore – that is why it's called "playing at work."

This then makes you one of the way-showers, and after us, the kids who come next will harvest those seeds of love. **Love** is the key word here. Obviously, we don't want to be sowing seeds of hate and fear! For, as you know and have witnessed, this does not lead to freedom. The time has come for the children to grow up in a new world of love, helping others in a different method and not a new world order of control and hate for sentient life.

WHO WE ARE

On a personal level, one can have a creed for himself/herself, talking about what you believe in and your resolve. You can have a battle cry for freedom, speaking about your unwavering faith and standing firm for those beliefs which are so important to you.

One can also have a prayer of gratitude and acknowledgment to God for all of the abundance and miracles. There can also be a declaration of intention for One's Self, affirming who you are and what you stand for.

My thought is that we could have a combo of all of these things that brings benefits for the whole world. It's time to let it be known, heard and said, not just for the sake of planet earth but the whole Multiverse. We are all one, everybody is listening! How about calling it our **Divine Freedom Intention and Declaration!**

After this, we will see what else we can do to anchor our true freedom! We have covered a lot of new ideas within this chapter. I hope you enjoy exploring and learning new information to help you begin to claim your freedom. Remember, all of this material has to do with **self-growth, self-empowerment** and furthering your knowledge base. The more knowledge people have that is true and correct, the more power comes to us for our **Freedom!**

DIVINE FREEDOM INTENTION AND DECLARATION

WE ARE: A divine spark of **God**, all-powerful **Souls**, and conscious light/ energy beings! Our name is **Divinity** and it is **Legendary and Eternal!** We are **free, limitless, and immortal!** We are omniscient, omnipresent and omnipotent, Hyper-dimensional hue-beings! We are masterfully creative, crystalline angelic beings with a wealth of ancient knowledge and manifesting experience!

We are here on a mission to promote peace, love, compassion and forgiveness while we continue our soul growth and cosmic lessons. We live under the planetary laws set up by and for the blue planet, **Terra!** We are here through a dispensation by this sentient being (our Mother Earth) that allows for the population to be here, engaged in a human journey of advancement along with Her to the status of a **Level One Galactic Planet**, that is transitioning into the **Fifth Dimension!**

Under the planet's protective atmosphere and Central Sun's source, we are a **Free United Republic!** We accept our free will and hold the **Law of One** as our motto, united under **Common Law!**

When our contract/journey has ended in the human vessel, we will either ascend or transition with our energy/over-soul into the Spirit world and prepare for our next form/experience.

While we are here, it is our **intention** to have **freedom** that isn't granted or taken away. We do not wish to engage in anything that isn't on the level of **LOVE/PEACE** for all, or anything that would keep us from advancing as a civilization.

This would include: Any type of cruelty to **Mother Earth's** nature and animals! Any type of tyrannical rule, corporations that place profit over well-being and sentient life. And or any type of negative agendas to stop or delay our evolving spiritual consciousness!

It is our intention to have not only freedom of religion/spirituality, but also of expression in our beliefs. As **we are all one**, we know that everything eventually leads back to the Source. We believe in the idea of **Ascension** along with the Earth, and calling in (contributing to the birth of a) **New**

Golden Age for the Populace! We, the people, believe in full disclosure of the Truth, knowing and having it for all mankind!

We understand that our success will come from living through our own value creation and authority. As we move into the next level of existence and sovereignty, we will know what it is to have true wealth in every aspect of life, and to live in peace. The heart of humanity burns with a Divine flame that is open to receive its **birthright!** We accept all of God's gifts of abundance with gratitude and love for all life that is evolving on earth. **WE ARE** awakened beings of light, grateful for all the blessings coming to us in this **Now moment!**

We are One with our I Am Presence!

and So It Is!

WHAT CAN I EXPLORE FOR FREEDOM?

www.keshefoundation.com   Recently, about October, 2015, the Keshe Foundation released their new free-energy device in the form of free energy power units. This is very important, not only because of free energy, but also for peace! The free- energy devices were given out to Presidents and Ambassadors. The idea was for them to sign the World

Peace treaty in order to get the technology. Then the blueprints will be released so every country can begin making their own. You may also enjoy watching the YouTube video for the 80th knowledge Seekers Workshop. Please see the You Tube channel for the Keshe Foundation under name given above, other videos available if interested.

www.ashtarontheroad.com This relates to what I mentioned earlier, which is **NESARA: NATIONAL ECONOMIC SECURITY AND REFORMATION ACT.** This covers a lot of issues concerning our freedoms, such as: Abolishing the IRS and Federal Reserve bank; releasing all the patents and information on free energy technology; full disclosure on all information regarding UFO's and beings from other planets and civilizations in our solar system, galaxy, and universe; debt elimination on any type of loan due to fraudulent practices; currency evaluation/asset-backed currency with precious metals, and a whole lot more. Look under the heading for history of **NESARA**. Also see the **Tara and Rama Reports** for news and archived articles.

www.pathwaytoascension.wordpress.com This is another good site for information pertaining to **NESARA**.

WHAT CAN I READ AND WATCH?

www.instinctbasedmedicinestore.com On this site you can find the book *The Only Answer to Tyranny* (Dr. Leonard Coldwell, 2010). This goes into detail about what it truly takes to live free of tyranny in all its forms.

www.divinecosmos.com This site has articles on financial tyranny, divine intervention and disclosure, plus free videos to watch.

www.freedomclubusa.com Another excellent site for knowledge dealing with multiple pillars of freedom, with a wealth of information to explore.

www.thrivemovement.com For governance solutions, the *Thrive* movie is also good to watch.

Chapter Ten

WISDOM

"It is unwise to kick the Golden Goose, laying the Golden Eggs, in the head! As one may never know the Wisdom he or she might bestow upon you."

What comes to mind when you think about **Wisdom**? Maybe you picture a wise older man or woman, a world traveler who has picked up all kinds of knowledge because of their travels and people they have met. This person may even have found a way to access ancient lost knowledge. An example might be information about **Atlantis/Lemuria** and our connection to past civilizations. But, in fact, you too have the ability to uncover the wisdom of the past because it lives within each one of us.

A part of wisdom is understanding that we already know everything we need to on a soul level. Our task is to **awaken** and remember what has been forgotten. One way to help this along is to put our heads together and form a **Master Mind (great minds thinking alike for a single purpose)** in order to capture the memories stored away inside us in the best way we can. The mastermind is achieved by us coming together with a common goal in mind. Think of seminars and workshops where a type of group coherence is formed and utilized to help manifest your goals. So, let's take this book that you have in your hands for example. The common goal would reflect the reader(s) desire for a bigger/brighter spiritual experience, more wisdom and the desire to remember what we already know, for himself/herself and the planet. With this goal in mind, just you by yourself or a small number of us can be extremely strong and effective let alone a large number to millions and so on. People can utilize the makings of a master mind and be a thousand times more powerful because we are on the same vibrational wavelength and focusing our energy for the purpose of spiritual growth in every area and to manifest our positive creations.

Another part of wisdom is integrating past/old knowledge into newly learned/acquired knowledge to reveal a new possibility or future timeline. It is not necessary for one to have visionary or precognitive abilities to see, or a better word would be, comprehend, the future. Our intentions are what matter most. If you have or create a positive cause, it will bring on or create a positive effect. The same is true for a negative version. Since there isn't any fixation to the future, meaning that we deal with high and low probabilities of trillions of outcomes, we are free to create the future in anyway we see fit. This is why we want to create in the most positive manner possible, so the effects keep mounting for the light and spiritual growth.

UNDERSTANDING WISDOM

The **Golden Goose** quote above is very special, and I have known this for a long time! Everybody can relate to this in one way or another and it is wisdom central! I consider it to be very important knowledge at the basic level – this is where everything in one's life begins and branches off! There is a saying: "God gave you two ears and one mouth, use them proportionately." What does that mean? The easy answer is, listen/learn more and know when to shut up!

A step further is, if you are talking too much you might miss the **Golden Eggs** right in front of you! People come into our lives, sometimes for brief periods of time, in order to teach us something and then they're gone. But that brief encounter could change your life forever!

The **Golden Goose** represents anybody who is of the light or a **light bearer,** doing their best to spread positive knowledge on the planet. Someone who is also caring, compassionate and trying to spread the love. This is anybody who has been beaten down and still gets back up, never turning to the dark side – these are the light workers, the way-showers, and the whistle blowers.

The **Golden Eggs** would be the little nuggets of **truth, knowledge, and wisdom!** Once we learn this, we realize it is unwise to step on or kick anybody in the head in order to get to our destination in life. You never know who they may turn out to be and how they could help you, and/or vice-versa.

This goes along with looking for the gold. No matter where you are, even if things seem bad or negative, you can always look for the positive aspect of the situation. The wisdom comes out of sifting through the dirt to find the gold - the shiny diamond/ruby in the rough terrain, or a bright pearl in a sea of filth.

HOPE

Some people think hope is for losers. Who are these people? People who don't have any hope, I guess! I have come to see that **Hope** is a key to knowing happiness in life, as is **Faith**. Both are actually very powerful.

When someone is stripped of everything and is having trouble even dealing with reality, the next step could be suicide. Hope might be the only thing left to hold onto. Hope is the light in the darkness and then having faith in the unseen can lead one onto the pathway out of hell.

If the people who came before us, the forerunners and trailblazers, had not had hope and faith, we probably wouldn't be here today. So, when all looks grim, first you need a little hope and then some faith!

When you have a knowingness that everything will somehow work out in your favor, even though you don't have all of the puzzle pieces to see the full picture, this is **Faith**!

TIME

Another interesting concept is the whole aspect of time. We must understand that there isn't any such thing as time and everything is happening simultaneously in the now moment or the still point of the **now**!

Still Point is a better name for time because it deals with the eternal nature of an invisible thread that connects all there is in the universe. The idea of time implies a fixed point, as if it could end. In reality, there isn't any "End Point," only a **"Still Point!"** So, one could gather/say that the only thing everybody totally shares, in the whole multiverse, is **Stillness!**

The way we have been perceiving linear time is through a **state of consciousness** from our third dimensional perspective (or **3DP**). Once we ascend to the fifth dimension and beyond, **time** won't be a factor anymore.

At this point, we use time in the third dimension like a tool, if you will. We need to track time in order to gauge progression from a linear stand point in the process of us moving forward. The whole act of **rushing** is a good example of this. I consider this also to be very important **wisdom!**

Rushing comes from us not understanding time and thinking we are going to run out of it. We have managed to put a clock to something that doesn't exist. One cannot run out of something that never existed in the first place. But what we can do is use the time we have **wisely!**

This makes the whole idea of "Rushing Time" a type of misnomer. Time, deadlines, and the clock are helping us navigate the third/fourth dimensional existence. It does not follow/make sense in terms of trying to rush something that doesn't really exist in the first place. Now, we don't want to self-impose a race with ourselves or other people. Healthy competition is good but not when it leads to separation. So, what do we do? **Wisdom says: Learn time management!**

The timeline or time thread is acted upon as if it is fixed, but in true reality it's just an avenue that has been or could be chosen. It is good to set goals and try to reach them in a timely manner, but trying to force a pathway doesn't create the result you are wanting. True time management involves taking action from a now moment standpoint, where you **accelerate with purpose instead of rushing!**

In our day to day lives, it is good to map our movements in such a way/form that we complete a series of goals that move in a natural flow toward the end goal. For example, I was in the flooring business for over twenty years. To get the jobs done in a timely manner, I had to perform a sequence of operations where one process was completed before moving on to the next. The end goal of the job was always a completely finished product/ floor, with installing and sanding and finishing as goals that unfolded along the way. If I was jumping around from one process to another all out of order, the job would have been very sloppy and nothing would have gotten done in a timely fashion.

As you progress forward and drive your purpose along in business/personal or hobby/passion, remember to go at it with your physical movements in line with your goal. This way you are in the now moment and not rushing yourself. You won't be stressed and you can make adjustments easily as needed.

Also, trust in your own **divine timing/internal clock!** Remember: One does not need an alarm clock to be reminded of the fact that **rushing yourself will only lead you to an early grave!**

Now, I know what you are thinking, and the burning question is: If all time is now and happening simultaneously, why can't we see our own progression, forward movement and everything going on around us? To understand this better, we must talk about something called, **Clear Seeing** – or you could call it **soul sight!**

WINDOWS TO THE SOUL

The eyes are the windows to the soul... We have all heard this and it's true – but why? All souls on a higher plane of existence, such as on **Venus (Hesperus)**, have **psychic clairvoyance** as a normal state of being.

This allows them to view everything that our human eyes can't see, such as astral projections of people/souls, and other amazing things.

We would call this supernatural! The thing about it is, the natural part is in all of us – these are in fact our **natural** abilities. The super part has been forgotten and buried in a heavy/dense third dimensional time construct, which means these are our **lost** abilities.

The window represents the human eye on the physical plane, and we use this eye as a tool to see the reflection of ourselves moving through this third dimensional reality. The reflection only goes as far as our current state of awareness - the point we have reached at any particular time.

The indigenous peoples are a good example of this. When someone doesn't know about flying crafts or airplanes, these things may be flying overhead for some time and still cannot be "seen" by them. Because that idea has not been a part of their world, it's as if it isn't even there. And then one day, after things are explained to them, an airplane pops up suddenly into their awareness and is seen for the first time. The ability to see the airplanes would spread quickly through the tribe. Everyone would be shocked and amazed, even though these craft have been around for a long time.

This is why we really don't **see** with our **eyes**. We create and view reality with our **level of conscious awareness!** On a physical plane, matter has to be in our awareness before we **see** it. This is also why we've been so adamant about, "I'll believe it when I see It!" We don't need to see to believe. The belief can come through a sense of knowingness, and after the awareness is raised, the **seeing** will commence.

We get the fire in our eyes with accumulated **peace and wisdom.** The **fire** resembles peace with the unknown knowledge and has **deep ancient wisdom** as its contents. This would be **soul love and energy** on a higher plane.

Speaking of a being on a higher plane... If a person were lucky enough to look into the grayish/blue **eyes of Jesus**, what do you think they would see? He or she would see endless/unconditional **love** from a **pure soul**, **(A highly advanced being with psychic clairvoyance)** gazing back at them!

What we're getting at here is that **physical matter can't reveal or see the soul!** Most human beings are very limited because they are identi-fied only with physical eyes and ears, which is easy to do while in a third dimensional vessel. Anyone who is in physical form is naturally focused at a lower vibrational level and can't see or hear things past there vibratory rate.

So, the matter **(Physical Eyes)** won't reveal or be able to see soul energy – something or someone that is on a higher vibrational plane of existence. Only with **clear seeing** can one look upon and hear things that are unknown to the physical human senses. Now, the good news, is that we are not talking about being special or born with this/getting it somehow, we are talking about all of us evolving into our higher-self and gaining back/ remembering our already earned skills. You will be happy to know that we are moving rapidly towards this in the now moment!

Now, I have a little treat for you! It's a story that goes along with our exploration of wisdom, and it's all about learning **now** from our younger self. After this, we will talk about some good things to do in order to keep expanding your personal **wisdom!**

WISDOM: FROM THE CHILD OF THE PAST

Back when I was about eleven, my little self was just arriving at the boy's ranch in Indiana. The place was pretty big, the business was farming and there was a lot of land. There were lots of things to explore, big house, farmers' market, cows and other animals, tractors and all kinds of stuff for a kid to do.

I was a so-called "ward of the state" in the foster care system, and since I was a kid, I basically didn't have any say about anything that was happening to me. To be honest, writing this now is for a greater purpose which is to go back and find the wisdom from myself when I was younger.

I want to share it with you, but it isn't easy, to say the least. It is very hard to bring up all of the hurt feelings from the child of the past. When I think about it, all of the lost and abandoned feelings are still there. Interestingly enough, with writing this, I am just now realizing how deep the emotional pain is.

This is very important because everybody has that child of the past within them screaming out to be heard.

So, as the foster parents were showing me around, guess what my main concern was? Where is the T.V.? I liked to watch my cartoons on Saturday!! I found the room with the **T.V. (telling you to program with your physical vision!)** but I didn't know that or care about that at the time. I just thought of it as an escaping reality treasure and I was a happy camper!

Unfortunately, my happiness only lasted about a week before I had to go out into the fields to work. Now, I already knew enough to know this wasn't right, but It had a much deeper meaning to me than, "This isn't fair." I was just denied being able to go back home to be with my mom again, so my cartoons were literally the only source of joy I had left.

Needless to say, I was very mad, lost and confused! Worse than that, the act of stripping from a child his joy and everything he loves started the closing of my shell after that point.

Work is another version of somebody saying **"NO"** to you. I have never liked that word and cringe a little every time I hear it! This reaction comes from the **"DREAMER"** trying to remember his or her highest excitement or something that brings them a lot of joy.

Remember hope? Watching the cartoons, at that point, was my hope! As bad as things were for me, at least I had them for some kind of light to lead me out of the nightmare I found my young/little self in and didn't know how to handle or get out of.

When you're an adult, you can have faith. When you're a kid, all you know and can do is shut down, go into a shell like a turtle and you don't come out until you know it's safe.

So, it is the same as laughing in your face as an adult, saying wake up! It is time to feed the greed machine and earn money. This is why people turn into "Workaholics." They are lacking joy and work a lot to cover it up, keeping themselves busy.

This goes along with what we were talking about in the freedom chapter. Now, at that time, as a kid, work didn't mean anything to me. All I knew at that age and the only thing relevant was that, it is time for He-man and the Thunder Cats to come on and this work business is messing up my plans!

As a kid, you shouldn't be rushed into working - or as an adult, for that matter, either. You want to have fun, play with your friends and enjoy yourself. As a kid, the highest excitement might be cartoons or playing. As an adult, pretty much the same thing! Your highest excitement, or the thing that gives you great joy, shouldn't be denied! The kid in you is saying, let's enjoy life, stop rushing, slow down, and stop to smell the roses! This translates to I want to go fishing, I want to go on vacation, or I want to play sports. This is very important, as these things not only give us great joy, but are also what we need for soul growth!

Too much work hinders that growth! Remember, you are the **Golden Goose!** Don't let anybody or anything **steal your dreams**, rush you into things you don't want to do, or, most importantly, **kick** you in the head and kill your **joy!**

Now let's talk about what to do for some more great **Wisdom!**

WHAT CAN I WATCH?

www.gaia.com There is a show on here called *Wisdom Teachings*, with lectures on different subjects like energy and the universe.

WHAT IS GOOD TO READ?

The Synchronicity Key (David Wilcock, 2014) is very good and talks about how history relates to us through time.

The Laws of Life (John Marks Templeton, 1998). This book offers a sampling of wisdom/spiritual teachings and principles from around the world.

WHAT CAN I LISTEN TO?

www.joedolezal.com and www.thepyramidcenter.org On these sites, there are good lectures on subjects like time, as well as other esoteric knowledge. Both of these sites have a lot of good articles to read. You can learn about the Pyramid Center, which is a spiritual retreat/resort, and listen to interviews on radio shows.

Alternative internet radio shows are a great outlet to utilize for knowledge and wisdom. A couple good ones are: **Coast to Coast a.m.** and **Cosmic Vision News**.

Chapter Eleven

LIFE

VEIL OF FORGETTING

The circle of life are we! Did you know that life is a big circle? I'm sure you have a lot of questions about life, as do I. Hopefully, with all the discussions in this book, we are working some answers out. Did you also know that we start to forget immediately about the Source and where we came from as soon as we come out of the birth canal as babies?

In the mother's womb, we are happy and our soul is still connected to the Spirit world. At birth, we leave our real home and **the veil of forgetting** sets in as we enter into life on earth!

We come in crying because we know the **love connection** is fading fast, and then the questions begin. As we grow to adulthood and begin to face old age, we spend a lot of time just trying to figure out who we really are.

Then, we go out with a smile on our face because we/our souls know it's time to go back to **The Source** (our real home). In order to understand life, it is helpful for us to get to know our True Self/Soul and how we actually operate. We operate from a base/four body system that gets more complex from there. For our learning and purposes, we want to get an idea of the basics and continue on.

DIVINE INTELLIGENCE

One could say that the body is like a car and the Soul is the engine. Our bodies are very unique, made up with, and of, Divine Intelligence. We wouldn't operate very well at all without a soul, or if we had very little Soul Energy.

First, we need to have the form created **(The Body)** and then the soul comes into it **(The Engine)** to give it **(Us)** life and consciousness to be able to run/function. Energy and Consciousness are the keys to **LIFE** and the building blocks come from the **Ether** and our **DNA, which is the encoding system of our physical form.**

Consciousness coming from Source Energy creates form, form does not create consciousness!

The Ether/Source Energy, which comes from Creator Consciousness is what ties the elements together to create the form/body. Drawing from the elemental kingdom, our four body system (human body/form) is associated with these aspects from the Ether, as follows: The Physical Body represents Earth, the Mental Body goes along with Fire, the Emotional Body goes with Water and the Etheric Body goes with Air.

COLORFUL LIFE

Have you ever seen birds of different colors and wondered how they got that way? For instance, what makes a blue jay a beautiful shade of blue (my favorite color) or makes another bird red, like a cardinal?

Through-out the Cosmos, Life Creation has obviously been going on for eons. The creation of Life in different forms is amazing and we haven't even seen the half of it! From color to size and complexity this diversity is never ending. This Creation Energy is being orchestrated through Spirit and Consciousness to create all life as we know it in various forms. We have all learned about the theory of evolution in school, where everything was said to have evolved through a random process of trial and error. I believe we need to take a deeper look into the origins of life and under-stand how the main ingredients (Consciousness and Energy) make it all come together and work effortlessly!

The form, whether it is humans, birds or animals adheres to a DNA code. The type of colorful being that results can be very diverse and beautiful! So, within these building blocks of life, full of color and energy that is flowing through the consciousness of every form, what do you imagine is holding it all together?

Magnetism! This is the force that holds energy in its correct formation. Our Souls give off electro-magnetic energy. Soul energy has high vibrations

from different dimensional levels. Colors are also associated with achieve-
ments from our/Soul's past lives in other forms and we come complete
with lessons!

LIFE LESSONS

What do these lessons consist of, you ask? Only everything under the
sun and over the moon, continuing into infinity! But don't start to fret,
because we never really die, so we have plenty of time to learn what we
want to learn! One big lesson that we have previously learned and forget
when we are born into human life is the fact that **We Are Immortal
Beings!** We don't actually have to age or die, for it is unnatural. By the
time you get done reading this book, you will have a better understanding
why this is true!

Within this third dimension (or the level of dense physicality), we human
beings have been constantly adapting to new forms of energy/environments
that are constantly being recycled into different forms that become lighter
and lighter in density.

As we learn/awaken and become more, light filled, our vibration increases.
We grow wiser and keep moving forward, with a higher consciousness
we stop with negativity and begin to build/shape our lives with something
I like to call, **Positive Life Construction!**

What does it take to build a positive, long lasting and vibrant/healthy life? First, we need a deep/strong foundation in **Love!** Second, we need the upmost respect for all life on the planet on which we have anchored said foundation – which is, **Mother Earth!** Thirdly, we need life sustaining/giving organic and pure sustenance from said earth, to maintain our **Biological Vessel!** Fourthly, we need Source- connected/unified practices to maintain a fully conscious fifth Dimensional vibration and above, in said vessel!

What do you think we get to experience next? You are correct! We are telepathically on the same wave length (like we are supposed to be) and thinking the same thing! So, we will experience: **Biological Immortality Fueled by God's Love!!**

Next question – What does this look like? If you have noticed, people are becoming more and more interested in longevity. To make a long story short, our biological upgrades are going to come from unlocking our DNA. However long this takes, it will provide what we have been looking for all along. This is already happening right now with everyone on the planet due to us advancing with the planet, taking on a higher vibratory rate and going into the fourth dimension and higher. In the next section and final chapters, we will continue to discuss/explore more concepts about life and the evolving of it. For now, we can continue with some more helpful insights into life.

Remember the old saying, "How deep does the rabbit hole go?" We know that the hole could go on forever, forever and ever, and yes, forever! The thing we need to concern ourselves with is, "How long is the Frick-n' Carrot!" I'm sure Bugs Bunny is getting pretty old and tired chasing and trying to catch that thing! The point is, finding the answers to the lessons doesn't have to be hard; it's all about getting the message in the first place.

This brings us to one of the biggest lessons in life, and that is simply, **Don't try to Copy Life!**

TRYING TO COPY LIFE

We touched on **GMO'S** and corporations before. What we have been talking about is some of the structure of natural life the way God intended it to be. The copying comes from some corporations making clones or copying organisms/matter, which involves genetically modifying and making new types of organisms or material. We have to be very careful messing with things like anti-matter and genetic manipulations. Trying to play God is exactly what has gotten past civilizations in trouble/destroyed before. As we aren't the first to do this, we are just the next in line trying to copy life and missing the messages and lessons from past examples.

Now, of course this can be done and is being done. The noteworthy thing is that even though the copy looks alive – it might be pretty and appealing or functioning in a convincing way – it isn't truly alive without the Source and spark of Consciousness. **AI** or **Artificial Intelligence** is a perfect example of this. Here is another Golden Nugget of wisdom for you.

The spark of consciousness or God spark is known as a white fire seed atom which is carried by organic life and is an individualized aspect of God/Source that makes each soul unique. Any and all types of human made copies do not carry the essence of God, therefore they are not authentic and will not last!

Like we talked about earlier, if there isn't a Spirit coming in with a lesson, then it's just an empty vessel, which would be a corpse or dead body **(Soulless)** trying to play God. I am not claiming to have all the answers here and our main focus is human life for the topic of discussion but in some way it stands to reason that this would be true for all of God's creation, whether it be cloned humans, modified plant/food source, animal cloning/manipulation or elemental control by technology. This would lead to/is, mass producing **(GMO'S) / (CLONES)**, a dead organism and or fake carbon copies with bad/ego driven intensions at the expense of natural life and **Real Conscious Beings!**

I refer to entities of this nature as dark ones who have very little light, have no soul/emotions, negative beings who have managed to make it onto the planet and or a version of the same who is trying to copy life in service to self.

These beings pride themselves on being separate from the Source, as in not-of- God and trying to rule/enslave, with the goal of taking God out of everything from religion to morality.

A loving entity and real soul originating from God doesn't need to fake his or her way through life. Only a copy trying to pass off a false identity needs clever disguises for the purpose of fooling the people!

How many times have you heard sayings like: "For the National Will," "For the Social Good" and/or "For the Social Well-Being?" If this is truly for the populace and with our best interest in mind, then that is great, but not if it is meant in a manner for trying to convince the populace to get behind wrong-doing. These sayings can be used as clever deceptions preying on the good people's fears and hopes for safety and security. Meanwhile, a whole different plan for control of the population might be in operation, arising from an intention to exploit copied life and generate material worth!

We have all witnessed corruption hiding under false pretenses, and thankfully not everything that goes on in our world is like this. **God bless the loving people who mean what they say and say what they mean!!**

Caring for the "National Will" cannot mean forgetting about the populace while we do what we want! Caring for the "Social Good" is not depopulation for one's own nefarious agendas! Caring for the "Social Well-Being" is not feeding **GMO'S** to already starving people and children!

All of these deceptions are part of the Grand Illusion, meant to keep the focus off of the fact that we are: Interconnected, sentient individuals with God being-ness, who have a mind of unity consciousness, respect, love and compassion for all life presently here, working to evolve together as one.

CIRCLE OF LIFE

The evolution of Life on the beautiful blue planet has been and is full of wonderful mysteries. Whether you have been here before - been involved in multiple life times (including this one) or it is your first go around, it is all part of our life circle for the purpose of human and planetary ascension. Everything we go through is part of us living and learning at the Earth school. We go through challenges, deal with karma, record our mistakes/successes and then take it all back to the creator.

Then, we start again on a new journey; it might be Earth school again, or somewhere else. The circle of life never stops. You can think of it as a never-ending clock.

So, going clockwise from the top: First, we have challenges, connecting us to trials and tribulations through which we learn about consequences of our actions. Second, we experience karma, which is having to deal with the effects of our decisions that show up in our lives. Third, we have Soul growth from experiences perceived as positive or negative, success or failure and right or wrong. Fourth, we take that information from our life experience back to the Creator, and then back to the top to embark on a new journey.

Once again we go on our way with a new set of challenges and as a new being. **(Please see diagram on next page!)**

After this, I have another treat for you to close out the chapter! Then, in the final section and chapters, we will switch gears again and get into some more interesting material that will expand your mind even further! So, I hope you are loving **LIFE** and enjoying our journey together! Take a break and remember the four **L's** for life. Life is for: **Living, Loving, Learning and Laughing!!**

CIRCLE OF LIFE

SOURCE/SPIRIT WORLD

Rest and heal the soul/light body, make a new plan/review options for the next journey. Choose conditions and body suit to start again/enter next new life.

EMBARKATION

EARTH SCHOOL

START: LIVING! LOVING! LEARNING! LAUGHING!

Prepare to Exit Old Life
Bring back information to the Creator

Challenges
Growth starts
Questions begin

Trials and tribulations
Forming Karma Transgression

Compiling Experiences
Positive and Negative

Gather Lessons-Pass on lessons learned to others

LIFE LESSONS FROM THE LLAMA

Speaking of learning and laughing! I saw the funniest animal behavior and their reactions to humans that I have ever seen at the Wisconsin State fair! I was about thirty-six and living in Wisconsin for a little while at the time. My girlfriend at the time, and I were strolling through the fair checking everything out. We both adore all animals and were very excited to see them!

We arrived at the animal section. There wasn't much happening with the animals at that moment – it was kind of quiet – so we moved through the area quickly. We came up where the llama's were. There were two of them together in the same area, facing opposite directions. They had their heads down, eating and minding their own business in the little pen area.

As we stopped to look, the one closest to us popped his long neck and head up, right at eye level with us. He had a funny expression on his face and he was drooling everywhere from eating!

He knew we were there, and he wasn't going to move until we did. He was very friendly but the look he had on his face was like: Why are you humans bothering me, you are interrupting my dinner, and what is so funny? Do I have something on my face? We weren't laughing at or making fun of the animal or being inconsiderate of his feelings, we were laughing because he was basically putting on a comedy routine as soon as we arrived, like he was waiting on us or something.

We didn't see food, just him steadily drooling and holding the same expression! He just stood there like that for a few minutes! Unfortunately, I didn't have anything with me at the time to take some pictures, or I would have put them in here for all to see, for sure!

We finally moved on, but we enjoyed our time with the llama. I was having a good time with my new friend! We made the rounds and wanted to see him again before we left, but he was gone by the time we came back.

I didn't realize it at the time, but I think this was a lesson from God about enjoying the little things in life. We can all learn a lot from the little things if we just stop sometimes and don't take ourselves so seriously. Because, just like the llama, one minute we are there living, laughing, loving, learning and the next we are gone!

WHAT CAN I READ?

Some good books to read that deal with life and our Soul's journey Include:

The Origin of Consciousness in the Breakdown of the Bicameral mind (Julian Jaynes, 2000).

Transformations of Myth Through Time (Joseph Campbell, 1990). Another by the same author is, *The Hero's Journey* (Joseph Campbell, 2014).

Journey of Souls: Case studies of Life between Lives (Michael Newton, 1994). Another by the same author is, *Destiny of Souls* (2001).

WHAT CAN I WATCH?

A good movie to watch that talks about energy and the universe is: *What the Bleep Do We Know*. A book of the same name is also available.

WHAT IS GOOD TO GET INVOLVED WITH?

If you want to get involved with something for peace and earth preserving organizations, check out: www.transitionus.org   This deals with setting up organic communities and towns. Also see: **Greenpeace, The Sierra Club** and **The Nature Conservancy**.

SECTION THREE

UNVEIL THE AWAKENED SPIRIT

Chapter Twelve

DIVINE FEMININE/MASCULINE

SEARCHING FOR YOURSELF

Divine Feminine and **Masculine** = **YOU!** We are females and males who come from a long, long eternal line of divinity (**Pure Souls**) straight from God's heart. You have probably heard a lot of talk about twin flames and soul mates. As you know and have seen, it can get pretty confusing if you don't know and understand exactly what this means.

Have you ever wondered where the constant searching comes from? It comes from maneuvering through life focused on the wrong things. **The list of expectations** is a good example of us following our head instead of listening to our hearts! The needs and wants usually come from a set of pre-programmed beliefs and desires, leading to a chain of disappointments.

As we pursue this avenue, the experiences that result set up a revolving door, and we never quite find what we are looking for. So, what are we looking for, exactly? You are going to be shocked and amazed at the answer! Wait for it...wait for it... **Your Divine Self**!!

Now, I know what you are thinking. **Holy crap, that's great! But, what the heck are you talking about?** Okay, I know you're excited!

But, we'll have to continue this discussion at a later time – **I have a hot date!** Just kidding… let's explore our Divine Self, shall we?

DIVINE SOUL

When God is in the creative process, a soul is born from an **orgasmic** explosion of **LOVE** that is released as a divine spark from God's heart. The new soul that is one, then splits into a divine pair, which of course, is female and male. (A soul can take on any form in terms of female or male but is usually partial to one or the other.) This pair is the **Twin-Flame**! The two soul parts, even though they are one, now have individual streams of consciousness. At this time, the departure kicks in and the female/male aspects of the soul go on their separate paths to learn, grow and experience. This is basically a crisis time where both souls are in the process of transfiguration. This has to do with our souls evolving in beauty, strength and power. The souls, even though apart for a very long time always remain connected, are with one another and can be called upon for love and assistance.

The time spent away from God and wholeness could be a very long time – millions or more lifetimes. A soul that has been around that long would be considered an **Old Soul**; a soul that has been around for thousands of lifetimes would be considered a young soul.

So, the Twin-Flame pair are the same energy and can technically never be apart but this is where the feelings of searching begin. The good news is, our Twin-Flame is always with us as that Energy Spirit, watching over us and vice-versa. The bad news it is rare for twin souls to incarnate at the same time. If we are on earth as female or male, then our other soul part is either in the spirit world or in another realm having learning experiences of some kind.

As you know, while we are going through and experiencing these lifetimes, (**Remember the Life Circle**) we are creating karma. It is hard to avoid piling up Karma (the result of the Law of Cause and Effect, or Action and Reaction), and only highly advanced/evolved souls can do it. Karma plays an important role in guiding us back to God and wholeness.

We learn from experiencing the results of our actions in the third dimensional reality as variations on the same themes play out, helping us grow.

Before we can meet our Twin-Flame again, we need to be on the plus side of resolving our accumulated karma. This has a direct connection with **Ascension**, because both flames must evolve in the spirit, and one can't become whole without the other. This has to do with spiritual expansion and everyone heading back to oneness with vibrational frequencies matching up.

What does all of this mean exactly? Remember hearing about "**A marriage/match made in heaven?**" Okay, at our Divine Essence, every soul/being has a **Twin-Flame** he or she is trying to reunite with to become whole and one again. The two separate energies coming back together again in harmony would be the **Holy Union**, which would be in the Spirit of God and **Heaven**.

Finally, together again back at the Source and Whole, the two soul parts would become androgynous and embody both equally, with karma at total completion. We would understand this as reaching a state of the Buddha, as himself and other spiritually advanced icons have been represented and depicted in teachings like ancient Hinduism. So, now that we are **Cosmically Aware** of this **Omni-dimensional** expression of ourselves, you can see and realize just how complex and **Divine** we really are!

SOUL MATES

Now that we are starting to understand more about Twin-Flames, we can talk about Soul-Mates. Since our Twin-Flame has the exact same energy as we do, we want to meet up with him or her if possible in any given lifetime. If this is not happening, we continue to hunt/search for that energy/vibration in a Soul Mate.

The difference between Soul Mates and Twin-Flames lies within the unique soul energy. We only have one **Twin-Flame** with the exact same energy signature as us, while we can have many **Soul-Mates**. While we are here on Earth, we attract and meet up with mates, that are souls who have a similar vibration to our own. A Soul-Mate doesn't have to be a lover or spouse; she or he could be a best friend or just someone close to us.

You may have heard the expression, "Soul Family." These are individuals who show up to play some role in our lives and have likely been on the path somewhere near us for eons!

Coming from a relationship standpoint, things have to be in line in order to attract a life partner or Soul-Mate. I am not claiming to be an expert on relationships, I am just sharing my findings with you. I have figured out, wanting/having companionship or being with a partner isn't about hunting down a Soul-Mate.

When you are of a like/positive vibration, you will attract the right person/people for you. In other words, through the Law of Attraction, we attract what we are, positive to positive/negative to negative. You have the power to change the energy YOU put out by making a conscious choice to improve yourself, but it will be like beating your head against a brick wall if you try to change someone else.

This little nugget of knowledge can save you a lot of trouble! Why? Because everybody is on their own path, working out karma and meeting people who will help them with their lessons along the way.

Soul-Mates come in many different forms/beings, with all of us evolving together. It is best to keep the focus on raising one's personal vibration and then, at the right Divine time for you, your Soul-Mate/mates will come into your life, and maybe even your **Twin-Flame**!

OLD WAYS CHANGING TO NEW

Things are changing for us rapidly. While the old ways were about exploring the forces of our animal nature and separateness — basically keeping our divine female and male natures apart — the new ways are about **Unity Consciousness** and bringing us together as one humanity in harmony with nature.

Our orientation in the past has been about competition for everything, fighting for and over resources and seeking power. It has been about the path of least resistance, looking for popularity, fast wealth and instant gratification.

As you have seen, this type of force has gotten us in a lot of trouble, pertaining to the world, and we have reached the stage (through the use of .

internet and the spread of information) where we can see and know the effects of our actions on a planetary scale.

We are finally noticing that the old ways aren't so appealing. It's like we have been there, done that and we now have come to realize that the negative dark road is leading to nowhere, even to annihilation of everything we love about this beautiful Earth.

Now, many, many of us want to experience the positive road and travel to the Light. With the vibrations of the planet getting higher and higher, the love/light quotient for the earth and for us is rising daily. This means that the negative action is falling away and we are moving toward an era of peace and love for all.

For those of us who are awake in this time and seeking a higher experience, we will be coming together and reuniting with our full Divine aspects. The **Divine Feminine** will be noticing more of her masculine traits and the **Divine Masculine** will be noticing more of his feminine traits. This isn't about taking one from the other; it's about realizing we are one in the same.

YOUR STORY

What is your story? I think it is pretty long for everybody, we are still writing it as we evolve, the answer is pending. The scenarios are ever changing and endless within the question. What would you like, the extremely long version or the short version?

The short part is, I can tell you about my life on Earth now as a Divine female or male. As for the long version, well…I will have to get back to you on that because I can't remember much more right now, living under the veil of amnesia. I'll contact you at **Ascension** time when everything becomes more clear!

And now, I have a special empowering treat for you ladies and men to enjoy! To wrap things up, after these little tales we will present some things you can do for more insight.

As always, the first part is for the ladies, but men, you can get your peek on too, and vice versa!

(Please see the following pages for your special stories!)

EMPOWERING YOUR STORY

DIVINE FEMININE – From Your Divine Self, for You

Hello Ladies! Did you know that you are the gate keepers? As Divine females, you are emotional beings and nurturers by nature. You have tremendous power to wield life-giving/healing energy and an amazing ability to transform- energy/matter.

Your power is known, and this is the real reason for the major suppression of females throughout time. It isn't because you were evil or witches, it was just more of the same mentality of people not understanding your Divine nature. Because of this misunderstanding and forgotten knowledge, women came to be viewed as a threat.

Unfortunately, throughout our known history, every measure possible has been used to keep you down. As a woman, you don't have to achieve a high station or have influence on society and the world to be considered a threat. "Who am I a threat to?" you say.

You'll have to take your pick on this one: male supremacy, egotism, war mongering **(Can't have war when female mothers want peace!)**, organized power structuring **(Can't have dominant monopolies when the ladies want equality!),** hate breeding, resource squandering…etc.

The point I am trying to make is: know and claim your worth - you are beautiful, Divine Beings of light! **Do not ever give your power away!!** Now, you probably would not knowingly/willingly give it away.

This is what happens when you fall prey to victimhood, which has been at the root of perpetuating of said situation. How are you going to let your beautiful, Divine light shine?

Have you heard the little expression, "The sun will never shine on you?" This simply means that if you are coming from a negative/victim standpoint, you will be kept in the dark and your light will be unseen. Everybody wants their light to be seen and recognized as the Divine Being that they are.

So, what do you/we do? Remember how we were talking before about looking for the gold and focusing on the positive, not the negative? Whatever is going on in your life right now, or happened in the past for you personally and all of the **Divine Feminine, Let it go, forgive and move on!**

The past is over. Know from this day forward, there will be no more suppression of the **Divine Feminine!** Think of everything that has gone on before as a very, very long experiment. Yes, it was, and it has been rough, but it is over now!

There is an affirmation you can do for yourself that is very empowering: "My name is so-and-so and I have never had a bad day." We can do that on behalf of all of the **Divine Feminine** across all time/space and realities.

So, repeat after me **(Men input Divine Masculine)**: **MY NAME IS DIVINE FEMININE AND I HAVE NEVER HAD A BAD DAY!!!!** Make this your new solid foundation and know that it is unshakeable! Trust in yourself and know that it has been sealed by **Mother and Father God**!

DIVINE MASCULINE

Hello Men! Did you know that you are the mentors? As Divine Males, you have physical strength and are teachers by nature. We, as males, have a tremendous power to build not just structures, but the actions of directing and leading life.

The subversion of the **Divine Masculine** has taken the form of men leading other men and women down the wrong path. This has to do with service to self through a destroy and dominate mentality. Just like the females' emotional nature has been subverted and turned into servitude, slavery and belittlement. Man's physical nature has been used for the purpose of trying to control nature and others through the use of force. In this way men have been the expendables.

Mankind (**On Earth**) in the third dimension – at least in our recorded history -has never lived by means of a natural flowing with nature, the Universe and himself. Throughout time (since our fall from grace anyway) man has been bred/taught, prepared/acclimated to fight for everything, (**even in schools**) instead of acting out of **Love** and nurturing the abundance of all.

Here is another little nugget of knowledge that shows how and why things got so out of control. This comes from a very weak, non-visionary mindset that uses man as pawns to perpetuate a false reality drawing from nefarious agendas designed to control through competition and subjugation of opposition until the bitter end.

There can't be war when fathers want to teach their children about love and spiritual thinking! Can't rise up and evolve quickly when man is brainwashed into thinking he is separate from God and everybody else!

The good news is man is finally evolving out of this mode/mindset! You are also beautiful, light beings! **Do not let anyone use and abuse your power!!**

How is this ever going to happen, you ask? It is occurring now through a new mentality of visionary/integrated thinking for the betterment of mankind. As in: Not following anything or anyone into organized agendas for the purpose of controlling multiple outlets.

This includes: Nature, women, man, land, resources, other biological life or created environments. This is the true meaning of us controlling our destinies. Our job - or better yet, our agreement - isn't to rule life and the planet.

Our responsibility is to progress life with value creation coming from the next level of human consciousness and love! It's about creating unity to bring forth the new. Know that there will be no more suppression of the **Divine Masculine!**

The act of a mentor is to open the apprentice to receive knowledge in a way that stimulates the being to bring forth creations in the world that are new. This comes from the person/student being liberated from stagnation, suppression or an unfortunate situation that they were once in. At this point, the teacher isn't needed and the student becomes the teacher, continuing on and on.

Everybody has an **I Am Presence**, and this is all you need for directing yourself, business and life. This Higher Presence is a guide to keep you safe and light your path so that you can be the best being you can be. Know that you are bringing about positive change!

As you enter this higher level of new thinking, you will see with new eyes and hear with fresh ears, in new ways. The Divine Masculine can use love energy to create values and find new ways of living that will benefit all beings. Just like the Divine Feminine, you can use this for yourself as an affirmation and we can say it on behalf of all beings across all time/space and realities.

So, repeat after me (Ladies input Divine Feminine): I **AM DIVINE MAS-CULINE. MY *I AM PRESENCE* IS ONE WITH THE *I AM PRES-ENCE* OF ALL LIGHT BEINGS!!!!**

This can be your new solid foundation. know that we are all advancing into a higher level of Christ consciousness together, and it is backed firmly by universal law and **Mother and Father God!**

WHAT IS GOOD TO READ?

A couple of good books to read that deal with relationships, soul-mates and twin-flames are:

   The Vortex (Esther and Jerry Hicks, 2009)
   Eternal Twin-Flame Love (Shanna Mac Lean, 2006)

WHAT WEBSITE CAN I LOOK AT?

www.circleoflight.net This site has good information about the divine feminine and the divine masculine.

Chapter Thirteen

METAPHYSICS: The Laws Of The Universe

RAISING AWARENESS

Albert Einstein – a supreme genius (1879 to 1955) admired for his advances in physics – is quoted as saying that "Imagination is more important than knowledge." One may have acquired a lot of knowledge, but it doesn't help you or anybody else unless it is put to use.

All new ideas begin your imagination. Next, you start pulling in knowledge, and then you start using your increasing brain power to create. In other words, we are always using our imagination to apply the knowledge we have obtained in one form or another.

Einstein also talked about how problems can't be solved using the same consciousness that created them. This means, whatever the perceived problems are that were created in the physical realm, the solution won't come from using old (**Previous Awareness**) knowledge.

Solutions will come from a place of **newly raised awareness** within the **meta-physical**. Then, a solution is put into action to address the problem happening in the physical plane. This happens because we have the ability to clear the slate of our mind and be newly inspired each day, working through and manifesting our destinies as we move through life.

MERGING

Metaphysics has to do with highly abstract concepts. It is a philosophy that deals with the first principles of things. The nature of existence, being alive and the world in general. We want to explore the merging ideas – meta and physical.

The **physical** part (**Our Bodies**) respond to our thoughts and perceptions. A good example is your health, we have already covered some factors in the Health chapter. But the main thing I tell people for health advice is to simply stop talking about their health in general. What we are discussing now shows why, if you continue to focus on bad health or pain, you will bring more of it about. We need to do our best to stay focused on solutions and bringing out our best self and then that is what we will get! Our thoughts form matter (**US**) and everything in existence. We can transmit/receive, broadcast/record and get information in multiple ways, but the physical is our experience outlet. The experience can either be positive or negative - on a personal level or collectively.

We could call this our base to work from, or **station**, that is surrounded by an energy field. This is why are bodies are called a suit or vessel. When we have a good/strong energy field – which is comprised of multiple layers of subatomic energy - our body suit is strong also.

If we get harmed somehow, or experience trauma, our station gets damaged and energy blocks set in. If we didn't have a body to come into – when we come down from a higher density - we/our soul would be in spirit form observing until the time was right for incarnation.

The **truth of existence** is that **energy** is the only thing that truly exists in the whole multiverse. In other words, there isn't any physical nature to energy. **Our true nature is as Pure Awareness**.

Do you find this interesting? If there isn't any physicality to energy, then what ties us here? I am glad you brought that up… and you will be happy to know that I have a very interesting answer, as well!

This is where the **meta** part comes in. You can't have the physical without your soul/spirit/energy. The connection to the physical body is the **Astral Body** and it is the astral body that remains in connection with **Source energy**. This over-soul or higher part of our bodies is considered **absent** in our science which has defined us as purely physical.

So, our souls tie us to the physical and, you could say, we are a highly complex thought-form! **Meta/Soul Energy** merging with the **Physical** or **me-to physical**. Knowing and understanding that we are meta-physical beings, we can see where we stand now and where we are heading.

NEXT EVOLUTION

We know that our lessons in the third dimension have been all about duality and separation. Our next phase of evolution is going to put us on the path to Oneness and Full Consciousness.

This is a step up, or quantum shift, leaping forward and evolving right along with Mother Earth into the next dimension. The next dimension is the Fourth, but we will expand quickly, almost bypassing it, going on to the Fifth Dimension.

The term **Hue-being** or **God-man** refers to us (**Man and Woman**) making this leap of consciousness/higher awareness to become a being that is one with the physical.

You know, I was contemplating all of this because one could ask: What is the purpose of knowing all of this stuff?

We could look at it like this: **Everything that we go through in life in the third dimension under the veil of forgetting who we really are**

is just separation symptoms on a very, very long journey towards manifesting ascension!! Since we are the ascension manifesting, we could call ourselves humble practitioners of God and for God, who have gotten lost along the way!

As are consciousness rises, we become more awake and aware of our True Self. So, as we move along, getting closer and closer to being fully connected, we begin to remember.

This is a huge game changer! This is also why things are so crazy and **changing rapidly**! Time is a good example of this. In a way, it seems as if we are losing time somehow.

We aren't losing time and it time isn't speeding up. Our consciousness is. If you haven't heard about this, it is being called the quickening. This is why it feels like we have sixteen instead of twenty-four hours in a day to utilize.

You could say that our metaphysics (remember, metaphysics are apart from concrete realities/what we perceive them to be) are changing or coming around in away that we haven't seen in a very long time but also, in unprecedented ways and upgrading due to our overall evolution. Our true nature doesn't have anything to do with time. This is why we must start to perceive new ideas from a higher perspective and understand that they really aren't new, only forgotten by us. Our true manifestation power comes from us starting to believe in the Meta-physical that is us! Ascension is where we make history with our advancing physical being.

As our vibrations rise, we evolve on the fast track to full Consciousness once again. In turn, this brings on the **Ascension symptoms** that you are hearing about and feeling now.

Such as: Irregular sleep patterns and waking up between 2:00 and 4:00 a.m, noticing synchronicities and number groupings: 111, 11:11, 333, 444, 555…etc. Heightened senses: Hearing/vision (**Remember clear seeing**) starting to come back as we get lighter and drop the denseness.

Remember, **physical matter won't reveal Soul Energy, but clear seeing will reveal physical matter!**

So, of course you will have unexplainable weight fluctuations, changes in eating habits, body aches and pains…etc. A lot of things will be unique to you personally. The thing to remember that you aren't going crazy, getting sick or dying! Everybody is experiencing these things in one way or another as we continue on this journey of **Ascension!**

ASCENDED MASTERS

Understanding our new Higher Awareness that we are coming into starts from the concept and perspective that we didn't begin all of this yesterday.

Remember how we were talking about the Now moment?

Being in and aware of the Now moment, allows us to let go of the past. Since all times are now, it would be correct for us to say that what we were before, we will be again.

What is an Ascended Master? First I will share with you the complex version that you might not know, and then the easy version which you are very familiar with.

Ascended Masters are souls coming from realities that exist in higher densities and frequencies who have the ability to exist in all dimensions. These beings or hyper-dimensional Old Souls are **100%** linked and connected to the Source and can take on any **Imaginary**/conceivable living form.

An easy example we all know is **Jesus**! We will talk more about how this affects us in the next and final chapter. So, are you interested in **Metaphysics**?

I can say I have always been interested in Metaphysics (what is deeper, beyond the physical reality), but I haven't always known what to do, read or look into for more information. In closing, here is some mind candy for you and some things to look into. Enjoy!

In the spirit of talking about highly abstract concepts, one could ponder this: Definitions don't define us or who we are. At one point in time/space and space/time, the dictionary, full of words and definitions, was imagined and perceived into existence. As meta-physical beings, we are each our own unique definition, needing a background to work off of and through. This is why we chose to be a physical human moving through a Third Dimensional reality. Our true definition…

ETERNAL!

WHAT WEBSITES CAN I EXPLORE?

www.dolorescannon.com   On this site you can look into her type of regression therapy, called: Quantum healing hypnosis technique or QHHT.

www.umsonline.org or the new site: www.metaphysicsuniversity. com   If you are really interested in metaphysics, you can find a lot of information here.

www.stankovuniversallaw.com   This is another site to explore for more knowledge.

WHAT IS GOOD TO READ?

Some good books exploring our metaphysical nature are the following by Gregg Braden:

The God Code (2005), *Deep Truth* (2012) and *The Divine Matrix* (2008).

Chapter Fourteen

FIFTH DIMENSION

ORIENTATION

If you have reached this chapter and you have read everything all the way through, I think you are ready for its contents. This is the final chapter of our journey together so, please prepare yourself for it being a little longer because I have a lot of great information for you to enjoy!

We will be talking about some things that some people consider difficult to believe, or controversial. I personally don't believe or think that anything at all, no matter the subject, is controversial! We always have diverse ideas floating in the field of our mind – things that we see or hear or that people tell us – that appear to be "for" or "against" something. But as we ascend, we know that all this is just "contrast" and that is how our minds work to gain clarity.

As you know and have learned, sweeping things under the rug, not dealing with it, or saying let's just forget about it only leads to more troubles. Why do we keep our eyes closed and run around blindly hoping things will just go away so we can all safely live in the dark?

The key word here is **Safe**. We have had enough of fearful thinking and there isn't any safety in the **Dark**! Life, as you know, can be a very long, dark and unsafe existence without **light, truth, and love!**

Remember, you/we are **Champions**; we want the **Truth** and we don't settle for **Mediocrity**! Sometimes leaving well enough alone is okay, but not when we are striving to press forward into enlightenment. When we know things aren't right and that we have been lied to, we can't just shake our heads and say "it is what it is" and keeping going blindly in the dark. The message we want to get from that is: Things are not what they should be and the Light is absent!

EXPANDING THE MIND

Mind expanding issues unavoidably deal with challenging subjects at the crucial point in humanity's history we find ourselves in. Jumping right in, a new shared vision is needed for where we are headed. What needs to be known and dealt with is that this entire reality is an out-picturing of our collective thought; the new vision begins first in the mind/imagination. We begin by imagining a world we wish to live in.

As you have probably figured out by now, we are changing and evolving. In order to move into the **Fifth Dimension**, we have to raise our vibration, individually, and as a people, globally.

Instead of working from only two, three or even four strands of **DNA** activated, we are evolving to having twelve strands in operation. DNA carries our genetic information and has all of our soul's history inside. This means that as we activate more strands of our DNA, more and more of our abilities and spiritual gifts/ knowledge will be unlocked. Simultaneously, our bodies are changing to a crystalline structure that is more Light-filled and fluid, instead of heavy and dense like the carbon-based body.

A gradual reconfiguration of our DNA has been going on for a long time now. This has to happen gradually, leading us to full consciousness.

We couldn't handle all of the Light/Energy and changes at once. It would be too much for our bodies and we would explode!

The same concept applies for us not being aware of the many/multiple aspects of our soul existing in different dimensions. We only know about and concentrate on this one at present, so we don't get overloaded.

It is important to know and understand that with our Light Bodies and Crystalline Solar/Eternal Energy, this is: **Who we are and what we are capable of doing across multiple dimensions!** It can be exciting to know this, but we still have to focus on what we are doing right here and now!

You know that feeling you get sometimes of being, "Stuck Like Chuck?" We get the stuck feeling from being in the middle of trying to progress further, but we are not quite aware of how to do it yet. As we learn and integrate new knowledge, the path is revealed to us.

This is what it means when you hear, "**Go as far as you can see and when you get there you will see further.**" As we absorb new knowledge, our Light/Frequency rises and this helps to propel us as Light Beings on our journey in life and on our way back to the Source.

PAVING THE WAY

There are a few steps involved with our advancement to becoming a level one **Galactic Planet**. The **First** step has to do with what we have been talking about, which is gradually raising levels of Frequency and Awareness. A good example of this is the way in which our parents and grandparents paved the way for us.

Do you remember stories from your grandparents about how they did not have the luxuries you have today? Well, they didn't have the awareness that we do today either, but the knowledge has to start somewhere.

They pioneered our existence by passing on what they did know and have. This is why your son or daughter or people from the younger generation don't know what an eight-track tape is – nor do they care, for that matter.

The old technology, the past lifestyles, and the previous awareness isn't relevant to them or us now. It's important to realize that without their level of awareness, we wouldn't have what we do now in terms of new technology which has been created from a new level of awareness and a higher vibration.

The **Second** step has to do with us, as in you and me, mothers and fathers, right now doing the same thing for the next generation. We need to be consciously awake and prepared to do our part in paving the way for the children.

This has to do with us accepting our true nature and who we really are. As we gain Awareness, we come to know that there are countless others throughout the whole Multiverse doing the same work that we are, at different levels of advancement.

In our role as mothers/fathers and knowing we can be One Unified People, we want the children and all life to evolve faster and better than we did. The faster we are able to raise our vibrations, the more quickly humanity can move out of the anti-civilization currently in operation on this planet. The reign of tyranny and oppression will be left behind.

The **Third** step has to do with understanding that we aren't alone in this and we aren't without support. We can be optimistic about our future because the younger generation and the children are here to help us usher in the **Golden Age/New Earth**.

Clearly, since **2012**, the kids coming in have more of their **DNA** activated and have a higher vibration then the previous generations. They have a higher awareness, are more psychic and have a closer connection to the Source.

You might be parents to these kids, or even grandparents by now, and certainly you have been around them or heard about these special children through friends or acquaintances. These new beings have been referred to as: **Indigo**, **Star** or **Crystal children**!

If you are parents, I want to let you know that there is nothing wrong with your kids. Please keep them away from any kind of drug that is lowering their vibration and killing their creativity. These children are being falsely diagnosed with made- up disorders like **ADHD** because the doctors don't know how to handle the complaints of teachers and parents.

ADHD means Attention Deficit Hyperactivity Disorder. This is basically saying that your son or daughter's attention span (because of boredom) is at a decline and their high vibration and or nonlinear thinking isn't understood. Therefore he/she is labeled as hyperactive and not like the other children; the conclusion is disorder or out-of-order for the purpose of blending into society and becoming just like the others. Final diagnosis: You child is a problem, so we'll give them a drug to keep them under control!

Remember, people hate what they fear and fear what they don't understand. So, your beautiful, brilliant kid with a high vibration becomes labeled as weird and given a drug to calm him down and keep him in line.

The answer isn't to throw drugs at the symptoms and forget about the precious Light Being! These kids, and all children, need better creative and challenging outlets for their energy, with support for a healthy lifestyle and that is it! It was important for me to interject this because, as you know, the children are very important towards the future and **Ascension**! Now, we can move on to the next step.

The **Fourth** step is receiving a helping hand through contact with other beings/races who have a positive interest/influence on us. Such beings are already guiding and assisting us with our advancement into the **Fifth Dimension**.

At some point, perhaps, humanity as a whole will experience our real, **First Contact**. Full disclosure of all **UFO and Alien Existence** has already been underway for some time. I think the term **Alien** or **ET** is a very rude way to refer to these great beings who have a long history of benevolent association with Earth humanity. A better and true term would be Galactic Brothers and Sisters! Please note that we are not talking about being saved by them, it is about co-creation. We are stepping into our own power to save ourselves and being granted the assistance we have asked for. People like Stephen Greer and others that have been following the "star beings" are trying to make full disclosure happen. Unfortunately, their efforts have been interrupted repeatedly by the dark, but we are now entering a critical time where the truth must come out. We don't need to see ships landing and aliens marching out, we need positive progress without future delay. And as they say: "Let the chips fall where they may!"

Opening to our Galactic heritage is part of expanding one's mind/imagination – grasping the idea of other life out there in the Universe! Some people would say that it's hard for them to wrap their head around this.

But consider this, if you will: **Just as surely as I/we are standing here, living and breathing, there have got to be other beings alive somewhere else!!**

It would be considered extremely arrogant to think that we are the only self-aware beings in the Universe. The key to allowing this new reality is simply a person's level of awareness. As in, what are you willing to let yourself be consciously aware of?

STARTING POINT: THE HOLLOW EARTH

The starting point is about a gateway into new knowledge and an awareness level chosen to branch off from. I have chosen the Hollow Earth for us to get more familiar with because it represents ancient knowledge that is right under our noses. Multiple credible sources have been talking about Hollow Earth and Inner Civilizations for a very long time now.

The findings talk about all planets being hollow and if not habitable on the surface, the beings would turn to the inner planet to occupy and live. In our case, third dimensional human beings have been living on the outer surface and higher dimensional beings have been living under the surface. So, of course the idea is to get to know more and explore our very own hollow – Mother Earth!

There is a lot of evidence piling up and information available about many civilizations living in Middle Earth, some for more than twelve thousand years. These civilizations together are known as the **Hollow Earth Network**. The ones we are most familiar with are **Agartha** and **Telos** because the inhabitants are descendants from former Earth surface civilizations of **Atlantis and Lemuria**.

We are touching on just a few points here and later we will talk about what to read so that you can do your own exploring if you are interested.

What we are learning is that the people living in the hollow earth are already, and have been, at a fifth dimensional level of vibration or higher for a long time now.

They have a thriving society built on the values of love, respect and compassion for all life. They conduct their business from a **Universal Law** standpoint and by working with nature. The people are totally free and use the barter system to trade goods and services. Their highly advanced technology works towards the betterment of all, not just a chosen few. They also have a clean atmosphere. Clean air makes for pure water and food that is of a light density and high vibrational quality.

There are stories available about a few people from surface Earth who have had the opportunity to meet them. The most notable is a story about a naval aviator named **Admiral Richard E. Byrd**.

Admiral Byrd was flying around one of the **polar openings**, as it had been found that the **North and South pole are entrance points to Middle Earth!** Long story short, the plane went haywire and he was guided down with the help of Inner Earth inhabitants, and he was able to meet and visit for a while with them. **(Another huge energetic area and access point is underneath Mount Shasta in California!)**

Now, this was about **1947** and Admiral Byrd kept a journal about his experience. We will mention this later also, in suggestions of what to read.

So, I know the question in your head now is: Why didn't we know about this back then and sooner?

It is important to know that **Admiral Byrd** was known to be an upstanding guy with great morals/ethics and he obviously had a positive vibration himself. Otherwise, he would never have been allowed entrance in the first place.

As the story goes, Byrd was excited about his experience, as anybody would be, kind of like finding gold for the first time! So, he went to the pentagon to report his findings, and I'm sure you can guess what they said. **You need to forget what you saw and keep quiet on behalf of humanity!** Unfortunately, another example of government saying that the people need to be protected from the truth, when in reality the intent is to preserve the existing power structure. So, the information regarding this momentous discovery was covered up! This is just one example among many of information that has been kept from the public. But one can bet that our friends from inner earth have been keeping tabs on us and know about everything that is happening up on the surface.

Most of the information that we are receiving about the Hollow Earth Network is coming from **Telos**. A very loving being named **Adama**, who is the high priest there, is taking the role of being in front, if you will, to relay messages and pass along teachings to us. The Inner Earth people are very excited about openly meeting us with full disclosure! They are very loving in general and fully connected to the Source. We need to understand that the high vibrational people from Inner Earth want to help us as much as possible with their knowledge/wisdom and advanced technology.

Secrets, Secrets and more Secrets! This is all part of our journey. Better late than never, right?

As you can see, I have done a lot of truth seeking, and I have learned/figured out a lot of **Truth** about the secrets that some people don't want us to know about. Just like everything else, I want to share my findings with you!

Please remember, don't take this material at face value. Anything that sparks your interest or resonates with you can be your **starting point**! Then you can do your own **Truth Seeking! It is time for everybody on the planet to know the truth. No more secrets and lies!!** So, let's play catch up, shall we! After this special section, we will get back to the next part of our Fifth Dimensional Journey. **(Please see the next pages!)**

THE MOTHER EARTH LOAD

THE VEIL IS COMING DOWN! COSMIC KNOWLEDGE IS BEING REMEMBERED! WE ARE NOT ALONE!

MOTHER EARTH NEWS: What Is being talked about/revealed? What are whistle- blowers everywhere saying? There are multiple credible sources who are directly in the thick of things and are revealing the truth. Some are in the military or have a high rank who are privy to information, or they may be having direct contact. Other key individuals are involved in channeling higher dimensional beings.

Please see **www.michaelteachings.com** to learn about channeling. There are many people who are doing extensive research into what is truly happening on Earth. With the veil of **ILLUSIONS** coming down, all people are starting to see through the very long and heavy cover-ups. This involves extraterrestrial activity at various times in our Earth history, and the fact that humanity is receiving assistance of various kinds from off-world civilizations right now. The "powers that were" would like the populace to think that everything is business as usual, because once the truth comes out about so-called aliens, the whole matrix of power and control will fall very fast, as it is doing now!

So, here is some information being made available to us. You can use your own discernment about it and explore more with the material I have provided in the questions section.

We have been/are being protected and overseen by many higher density beings, such as **The Silver Legion**. This is a group of beings from multiple races across the Galaxy with many different skill sets. They are helping us prevail against any negative forces and are considered to be **Warriors of the Light!** Also, here under what is known as the **Ashtar Command** is **The Galactic Federation of Light!** This is an Intergalactic Federation of benevolent extraterrestrials composed of many different civilizations that are millions of years beyond our current level of advancement.

With Earth's pending **Ascension**, all would be inducted into this galactic federation as a level one **Galactic Planet**. This is why a federation having a large number of starships/motherships is in our vicinity now. It makes sense that the personnel of these ships are the beings from these civilizations who are currently observing, protecting and helping to prepare us for our coming advancement.

Some of the civilizations we are developing relationships with that you might have heard of are: **The Arcturians or Lyrans, The Andromedans, The Pleiadians and The Sirians**, to name a few. We know about **The Sphere Being Alliance**, which is also here assisting us. They are an assembled, non-violent group here to spread a message of love, peace and service to others. The ones we are not so familiar with, to name a few, are **The Blue Avians, The Orb Beings and The Golden Triangle-Headed beings**.

Becoming increasingly major news is the secret space program (**where a lot of the world's wealth has been funneling into**) that has been going on for a while now. This deals with certain people (**again, with their own agendas in mind**) using advanced technologies (**that have not been released to or publicly known**) to create an interplanetary space station for an off-planet domain and/or base for travel. Having cloaking technology and ships with capabilities of interstellar travel, they can be used for multiple purposes, including trying to conquer and control other planets for resources. (**Once again, I refer you to our important discussion about clear seeing!**)

As the veil thins, all aspects of our Divine Soul begin converging and other realities on a higher vibrational level than our own will start to be seen. I believe personally that when the time is right and there is no longer a hostile environment on Earth, our **Galactic brothers and sisters** will come down in small scout ships to **PEACEFULLY** meet and greet us! The increasing sightings of lights and ships are them letting us know they are here and to basically break us in gently. I also believe that the benevolent beings who are here will not let a false invasion happen or allow anything/ anyone to interrupt our planetary ascension!

Our **Sun** – another big, conscious energy source – is playing a major role in this cycle of planetary ascension. Our galactic friends are helping to adjust the Sun's solar storms/flares so that it doesn't create disasters for us while we are in mid-shift with changing frequencies and moving into the **Fifth Dimension**.

These benevolent beings are also helping the whole earth with their technology to stabilize the **Bio-magnetic energy grid**. We have also learned about the **Andromedans and the Andromeda Council** having what is known as **Biospheres**.

These are hollow planets/ships for space travel that have been artificially created for a special purpose. These **Planetoids** can hold about two million people with full living environments and ecosystems. They have many of these very large spheres, and just one of them is close to the size of Pluto!

They are powered by a **Crystalline Fusion Generator** enabling a tremendous energy source. This is technology built using crystal and cold fusion energy that we are starting to get more insight into now. **Once free energy technology is 100% released and known, it will very quickly change our whole existence and way of life!!**

We would know and recognize these as **Dyson Spheres**, a megastructure that would harness the energy of a star, like our sun. With this technology, they are creating a shield around our earth and working to keep anything from coming in contact with us like the **so-called planet X or NIBIRU**!

The activities of benevolent beings helping us with this are also keeping the effects of earthquakes and disasters to a minimum as much as possible. Once full disclosure happens, we will get the truth and access to shared/gifted technologies. Also, know that every day people all over the world are waking up to the truth and fighting for freedom and unity. **No longer will Mother Earth and her people be condemned to a slave planet in service to evil and corrupt beings hell-bent on maintaining power and control!!**

Please watch out for disinformation, and keep in mind that any talk of doom, invasion or catastrophes is just coming from a fear mentality! We are already past the tipping point where there is more positive energy on the planet now than ever before and increasing daily. Until the time we awaken as One Humanity, our job is to learn as much as we can, keep asking questions and stay vigilant in our efforts to put the **Truth in the proper context for everybody!!**

THE FEMININE HARMONIC FREQUENCY

LOVE

DESCENDING THROUGH THE

COSMIC PLASMA FIELD,

IGNITES UNITY CONSCIOUSNESS

IN A NEW 26,000 YEAR CYCLE

OF PEACE!

PASSING THE TEST

How do we advance as a civilization to the Fifth Dimension? If we want to move on to the next grade/level, here at the **Earth School**, we must past the test! There are a few things to do in preparation, as usual. The big difference being, this is a global test!

Contents of the test include:

1. Whatever we do with our creative passions in life and the act of living should be in service to others. We can't score a high grade with personal and selfish agendas! We have got to work as a team/collective for the good of all.

2. Just like the parents and teachers who continued getting onto us at school/home, we have got to **stop fighting with each other!** We are not talking about toning it down a little, it has got to be completely. As in, no more fighting over resources, race, religion…etc.

    Does this sound hard or impossible? Yes, it may be easier said than done, for sure, but I have discovered that it really isn't that hard, my friends! It just takes major effort! It doesn't matter who you are, how crazy or complicated your life is, or what you do in life, such as: Rich/poor, high status/low status, old/young or station/nationality. At the end of the day, **we all have free will!!** You can be consciously aware of what is transpiring around you and make the decision right here and now that **I am not doing this anymore!!** Guess what? When this happens, your awareness and vibration shift to a new/higher perspective. This would be a Fifth Dimensional perspective (or **5DP**) instead of a third dimensional perspective (**3DP**). This means you are not thinking about war, fighting and separation. You are thinking/living love, compassion, unity and **Peace!!**

3. We, as one, must learn to work with the Universal Law and nature, working with the flow and not against it. We also (**As One**) need to learn the **Law of Consistency**. This is where all beings are taught and learn about everything, up to date, from birth. (Teachings from Telos).

    All beings should have equal access to knowledge, while co-existing as one! We are all entering new territory here, but the idea is about getting prepared for the next level of advancement. It is great to have a high IQ/high intelligence quotient, but that alone won't get us to where we need to be. We also, and more importantly, need an elevated LQ, which is a higher **Love or Light Quotient**. One doesn't have to be smart or a genius to be more loving and compassionate!

4. The next stipulation – and one of the biggest things we are evaluated on as a civilization progressing to the Fifth Dimension – is the way we

treat our animals. We haven't scored a high grade in this area, for sure! As soon as we show the level of love and compassion for our animals that our Galactic brothers and sisters show towards their animals, we will be able to meet them and their animal kingdom as well. With our advancing evolution, this means we won't be eating the animals anymore and they won't be eating each other. We also won't be corralling/caging them up for show, sport or amusement. All animals are precious living beings like us, and soon the **Lion will lie down with the lamb in peace!**

With all of us working towards positive change and raising the vibrations of the whole planet, we will finally be able to make the shift into the **New Earth, (Earth Two)**. With this next leap, we will be creating a much lighter density for us to live and grow in. Finally, after all this time, we will be able to mingle with and experience unending creations and joy from all walks of life together **as One!!!!**

Now, it is time for the final grand questions!

WHAT CAN I READ?

A few books about Telos, are:

TELOS: First Transmissions ever received from the Subterranean City beneath Mt. Shasta (Dianne Robbins, 2015)

Telos, The Three Part Trilogy (Aurelia Louise Jones, 2004-2006)

Books about Agartha:

The Smoky God: Or, A Voyage to the Inner World (Willis George Emerson, 2016)

Agartha: The Earth's Inner World (Mariana Stjerna, 2018)

A book on Atlantis and Lemuria is:

A Dweller On Two Planets (Frederck S. Oliver, 2017)

More good books to read dealing with other beings and the Fifth Dimension/New Earth include:

From Elsewhere: Being E.T. in America (Scott Mandelker, 1995)

A Wanderer's Handbook (Carla L. Rueckert, 2001)

The Custodians: Beyond Abduction (Dolores Cannon, 1998)

Keepers of the Garden (Dolores Cannon, 1993)

The New Earth. This is a three-part series available online at:
www.thenewearth.org

The Urantia Book: New and Improved (multiple authors)
Also at: www.urantiabook.org

WHAT WEBSITES CAN I EXPLORE?

www.DianneRobbins.com This is where you can read the article about the aviator interacting with the people from **Telos** and other civilizations also.

www.Gaiatv.com There is a show called Cosmic Disclosure talking about multiple subjects including: The secret space program, the Sphere Being Alliance, the Blue Avians, and much more. You can watch a couple of free episodes to see if you are interested.

www.siriusdisclosure.com The Sirius Film is highly recommended. A very important work exposing UFO cover ups, talking about free energy research and interviewing a lot of whistle-blowers with first-hand experience.

www.spherebeingalliance.com This site has a lot of information regarding the **Blue Avians** and their role in everything.

www.exopolitics.org There are articles and reports on this site about **ET** existence and cover ups.

www.silverlegion.org This site talks about how the **Silver Legion** got started and what they do.

www.andromedacouncil.com There is a lot of information on here talking about ascension, **The Andromedans**, various radio shows and people to listen to for the truth.

Chapter Fifteen

CONCLUSION

In this final chapter, I will share with you my thoughts on soon-to-become realities for all of us here on Earth. All this time we have spent, up until now, has prepared us for what is coming. We are learning about integrated thinking, how to be a self-leader and self-sufficiency. This is very important when we are looking within ourselves for the answers instead of outside. Now, we are reclaiming our freedom to explore life unencumbered. Finally, we are opening our eyes to the real world around us, realizing who we really are, where we come from, all the endless possibilities of the universe and just how free we truly are!

Our true heritage is long and Divine. We are beginning to understand that we all come from the same God spark! With this knowledge and knowingness, we can't fight our true nature anymore. It is time to truly embrace our Spiritual Self, Universal Law and living/ working with other beings here with us now and in the multiverse. After all the lies, cover ups and tremendous effort to keep people in the dark and down, one would think that we would be extremely hungry for the Truth in every form, no matter what it is, how small or grand! **I say, let's get the Truth and go with the flow!!**

NO MORE FEAR/WORRYING OURSELF TO DEATH

There is no sense in fighting over things today that are not going to be here tomorrow. Focusing on lack, outdated resources and material/beliefs of yesterday will not move us forward. Moving forward as one, we just have to be thankful for what we have and for everything that has gotten us this far. Now, it's time to integrate all of our old knowledge with the new and press onward into the unknown for the next chapter in existence!

We accomplish this by having open minds, putting the Truth in the proper context, with common sense and rational intellectual/intelligent thought. In believing in ourselves/others and most importantly, trusting that **Mother and Father God** will be right there assisting us in our efforts!

Let's leave fear and illusions behind and look at some things we don't have to worry about anymore!

- **Fossil Fuels** – Newly created technologies by us, released patents and technologies we already have, shared/gifted technologies from our galactic brothers and sisters, will make **Free Energy** available to all. This will leave out dated fossil fuels, draining mother earth, fighting over them and money slavery to them behind.

- **Food/Water Resources** – With our current knowledge on organic food and pure water, combined with new knowledge that we are learning from our friends in Middle Earth and working with nature, we will be able to grow and have plenty of food for everyone. The food source will be all organic food that still has the life force intact, not food that is considered dead. Switching over to a raw food/plant-based diet and majorly cutting out meat consumption, to soon – not at all, will leave the major strain on people for food production behind. This will also dramatically improve our health and longevity.

- **Fiat Currencies** – All banks will be what is known as **Basel Three Compliant**. Which means a stronger international regulatory framework. With the full enactment of NESARA Law, they will be asset-backed with precious metals and no longer using fiat (**Debt**) currency or corrupt practices. This will increase our buying power tenfold and ease the stress on people, in terms of debt slavery. With everything working together that we are talking about here, this will bring the wealth back to the people. This also will take us to eventually becoming a cashless society in the coming future, as in not using or needing money anymore at all.

- **Health and Well-Being** – We are doing really well in this department, developing natural and alternative methods for healthcare. This will increase with not only our new technologies but help from people like the **Arcturians** who are masters in the area of health. This is where we will be learning more about non-evasive treatments, energetic cleansing and fixing the source of health troubles. This will lead to everybody having **Dynamic Health** and eventually, as our vibrations rise to the fifth dimensional level, we will not be getting sick anymore. With this, diseases will drop off, along with our need for drugs and insurance. This will release the huge burden on society for affordable healthcare.

- **Crumbling Matrix** – The matrix or pyramid of corruption devised by the so-called "powers that were" is crumbling down with break neck speed! Our **Freedom** can't be denied and prolonged/delayed any longer. **Remember, nobody has authority over you unless you give it to them!** We are evolving to the next phase of our existence with the planet, where we will have newfound skills within our own self, which will bring on new creations. This will leave the need for a power structure behind and reconfigure governments according to their true purpose, which is **Protecting the Free People!**

- **Separation and Duality** – We are now in the early stages of the Fourth Dimension with old realities leaving fast and new ones coming in. As we quickly advance to the **Fifth Dimension,** we will leave duality, separation, negativity, ego, organized control of any type and most importantly, **Karma** behind! This means, **no more WAR and killing precious light beings and destroying planet TERRA!!**

- **Transportation** – Just like everything else, our methods of transport will change from individual methods/separation to much cheaper and efficient going towards free, fast and convenient travel for everyone. We will advance to having new propulsion systems and electromagnetic craft/vehicles for air and ground that operate with crystal/plasma/fusion energy causing no waste or pollution to the environment. Once we learn a lot more about working with the **Universal Law,** these things will quickly become reality. This will ease the thermal stress on the planet, remove our dependence on the wheel and crude resources to run pollution-causing engines.

- **Communication** – The lowest form of communication is actually verbal speech. Once our abilities kick in with full consciousness, we will be conversing telepathically. It is already starting to happen with people now as vibrations rise. This will leave behind our need for devices, cellular or otherwise that emit harmful electromagnetic frequencies and radiation that causes severe damage to the planet and our energy bodies.

- **Labor and Time** – We have been working harder instead of smarter. With our consciousness leaping forward, everybody will be working smarter and creating values for the world. This will bring on new freedoms for all of us and change the amount of time we are spending on labor. From this we will go to shorter workdays like: From **eight hours to six to four**. Basically, time cut in half, compared to now. This will bring on more time for us to work on our creations and have fun doing whatever we enjoy, leaving long workdays and weeks behind and the toll it takes on people due to stress!

- **Weather Extremes** – When the thoughts of the populace are at a steady and positive/loving high vibration, then the crazy weather from negative thoughts rising up will subside. Humanity working with **Mother Earth** will bring on a nice comfortable temperature for all and it will be consistent. The purging of negativity will be a big step forward in getting the Earth back to her pristine condition, leaving weather extremes behind.

- **Aging and Death** – Our long cycle in the third dimension was very heavy, negative and dense. Our **DNA** was basically turned off and became dormant except for a couple of strands. This descent we have experienced, dropping down to a lower vibration/density has put us in a degenerative state, causing us to have a brief life span experiencing many unnecessary ways to die, and causing us to become short in stature as human beings instead of tall. In other words, the beings we have become are unnatural in comparison to our **Natural** unlimited selves. Unnatural means we experience aging, leading to death. Unlimited means immortality and us choosing/deciding when we die/change forms and transition our energy. Now that we are on the upswing, heading to full consciousness with all of our **DNA** opening up, it will become the other way around like it is supposed to be. We will be living longer, we will have greater vitality, we will have lighter energy bodies with all of our Divine abilities coming online, and we will be getting taller with each generation. With us becoming fully conscious beings and going into the Fifth Dimension, we will: **Leave Aging and Death behind and be on the road to Biological Immortality!!**

These are just a few positive changes for the betterment of all going into the Fifth Dimension and Earth Two. There will be many variations and a lot more to come in the unknown, new territory we will be experiencing, I'm sure. Remember, **worrying is negative goal-setting and fear's best friend. Natural flow is positive creation and love's best friend!**

Well my friends, I want to say **THANK YOU** for coming on this journey with me! I'm sure you are as excited as I am to see the next level of love and peace that is already forming on the New Earth. I wish you the best and all the love and blessings from **Mother and Father God**. Please trust that all the struggle and heartache is coming to an end. Just like getting over a bad fever and delirium, we our cleansing ourselves and arising into the new energy of Love and Light! Finally, after eons in the dark, **WE ARE COMING OUT OF THE ILLUSION!**

Until next time, keep striving for greatness!

~ CHRISTOPHER MICHAEL LINK

IF NOTHING IN YOUR REALITY IS REAL

LEAVE THE ILLUSION BEHIND AND

PRESS FORWARD INTO THE UNKNOWN.

WITH AN OPEN, LOVING HEART AND

EXPANDED MIND, RECEIVE YOUR

BIRTHRIGHT IN A NEW REALM!

STIMULATION

Hello new friends and enlightened champions! I hope you have thoroughly enjoyed the book so far, but don't worry, I'm not leaving you yet! I've got lot's more! Wait a minute, I got excited there! Sorry, that's not PC!

I mean, I have more information on the following pages, if you so desire, that will assist you on your travels to expanding the mind and stimulating your curiosity, increasing your knowledge in this new age of information that will be beneficial for you and everyone you meet! There, that's better! Yes, that happened, nailed it!

So, think about a big party, with **truth** as our theme and stimulating conversation as our big topic/guest! I wanted to give you two or three more stimulating things to check out for each chapter.

All of the recommendations we talked about in the chapters is the best material I have found so far. So, you could call this the second best, but equally good and helpful. We will start with chapter one and go through them all. Okay, have fun exploring and being exposed to some new information!

ENERGY

The Secret (Rhonda Byrne, 2006). This is a good book to read that talks about the basics of energy and how it works in our everyday lives. The movie is also available.

www.ichingsystems.net On this site you will find information about alternative energy, health and well-being material, in a special system that was created to stop the negative trauma and energy moving through generation after generation.

HEALTH

www.naturalnews.com This site has a lot of information about alternative health news and good information on multiple subjects.

www.biocarehospital.com This is a good site to explore your options for health needs and can be good for, out of the country medical care.

www.boughtmovie.com This movie explores the truth about vaccines and **GMOs**. You can check out the movie or book.

www.helpingamericanow.com On this site you can find good Silver and Heavy Metal Cleanses and other information.

www.mercola.com   This site has an abundance of great natural health information. With videos, articles and other news.

WELLBEING

www.goldendoor.com   This is a very good option for travel/leisure and vacation.

www.chakrahealing.com   This site has good information on rebalancing and working with your chakras.

PASSION

www.maxinetaylor.com   This site has information and books on finding your passion and mission in life through special techniques.

www.superherotraining.com   On this site you will find information on how to unlock your true potential.

www.eraofpeace.org   This site has great information and products to help you find your true purpose in life, including the book:

Who Am I? Why Am I Here? (Patricia Diane Cota Robles, 2010).

SPIRITUALITY

www.in5d.com   This site has a lot of recommendations for spiritual books and other useful information on the subject of Spirituality.

www.omna.org   This site has a lot of information of a spiritual nature in forms of: Books, audios, videos and meditations. It also has channeled teachings within messages from higher Dimensions/Beings.

www.llresearch.org   This is the site dealing with the **Law of One** material and other information of a spiritual nature.

LOVE

www.attunedvibrations.com   This site has the solfeggio frequencies for love and healing tones to listen to.

www.joy2u.org   This site has a lot of information on love and ways to pass it on.

A great book to read is:

Whatever Arises, Love That (Matt Kahn, 2016). This is all about the huge Love revolution sweeping the Earth.

TRUTH

www.fluoridealert.org This site has information on the truth about fluoride.

www.seedsofdeception.com This site has more truth about **GMOs**.

www.dorway.com This site has the truth about **aspartame**, being a harmful toxin in sugar substitutes.

www.solari.com This site has multiple topics for the truth and up to date news. Please see, **The Solari Report**.

www.decalcifypinealgland.com This site has information about decalcifying the pineal gland. Look under theheading for: The Educate and Awakening Video Library.

A good book to read is:

DMT: *The Spirit Molecule* (Rick Strassman, 2001). This book is all about understanding The Third Eye and how it serves human beings.

Zeitgeist is a movie you can watch on YouTube about religion, politics and money.

SUCCESS

www.PeterWink.com This site has a lot of information on success and success strategies. A good book to read is:

Negotiate Your Way to Riches (Peter Wink, 2003). This book talks about strategies for negotiating everything, so you may acquire the best price for what you want.

One of the top recommended books for success and personal development is:

The Seven Spiritual Laws of Success (Deepak Chopra, 1994).

Another great book for success is:

As a Man Thinketh (James Allen, 2016). This book is about personal success driven by positive thoughts.

www.drwaynedyer.com This site has a wealth of information in the form of books, audios, articles and events to explore and utilize for your success.

www.simpletruths.com This is another great site for information on success with inspirational material.

FREEDOM

www.lightparty.com   This site has information on a new synergistic political party for peace and freedom.

www.projectcamelot.org   This site has a lot of information pertaining to freedom and truth for the world, coming from multiple whistle blowers with a lot of knowledge in their respective professions. Please look under the heading for Interviews and Reports.

www.deusnexus.wordpress.com   On this site you will find all kinds of articles, videos and freedom/disclosure information.

www.toolsforfreedom.com   On this site there is a lot of information to explore about freedom and reclaiming sovereignty for yourself and the planet. You can also get a catalog full of books, DVDs, articles and other resources that are hard to find anywhere else.

WISDOM

www.hiddenlighthouse.wordpress.com   This site is a great place to get more wisdom and knowledge on multiple subjects.

www.ronnastar.com   On this site you will find a lot of material that deals with wisdom teachings from Archangel Michael.

A great book to read is:

Bringers of the Dawn (Barbara Marciniak, 1992). This book is all about wisdom teachings from the Pleiadians.

LIFE

www.wiselygreen.com This is a good site for natural, toxin-free and green living information.

www.fixtheworldproject.org This site is about a humanitarian organization you can get involved with and has information on other good projects.

A good book to read is:

Universal Vision: Soul Evolution and the Cosmic Plan (Scott Mandelker, 2000). This book has topics that deal with teachings for Soul advancement.

Another good book is:

Many Lives, Many Masters (Brian L. Weiss, 1998). This book has information on the subject of reincarnation.

DIVINE FEMININE/MASCULINE

www.diamondheartflame.com This is a spiritually conscious site where you can awaken awareness. It has a wealth of information through articles and messages that have been channeled from higher Dimensions/Being to enlighten the Divine Feminine and Masculine.

www.7thunders.com This is a unique site with a lot of information on helping you find your destiny, for love or other insights to personal development.

METAPHYSICAL

www.cassiopaea.org This site has a wealth of metaphysical information to explore and read online. Please see the **Wave Series**, there are about eight volumes to read. This is very good channeled text like **The Law of One** series and it is recommended by the same author.

For more books of a metaphysical nature, please see: www.therabbitholeusa.com

Another great book to read is: **The Three Waves of Volunteers: And the New Earth** (Dolores Cannon, 2011). This book talks about Souls coming in at different time periods to help increase the light on the planet.

www.davidnova.com   On this site you can check out the book series called *Season of the Serpent*. These books are metaphysical fiction, put together with real synchronicity and correlations to life on the planet and in the universe.

FIFTH DIMENSION

www.treeofthegoldenlight.com   This site has a lot of material to explore and articles to read that deal with us going into the Fifth Dimension. Also, please look under the heading Other Wonderful Sites for more information.

www.teloschannel.com   On this site there are master classes for learning about **Telos** and other teachings to help raise your vibration to the Fifth Dimension.

www.andromedanlightwork.com   On this site you will find tools and information to explore ascension. Please see the heading **Light-bearers Journal**.

www.paoweb.com   This is the **Planetary Activation Organization**. On this site you will find great books, webinars and other information, new and archived. Also, they have regular updates for galactic news pertaining to the planet.

<u>www.shatteringthematrix.com</u> There is a lot of information on this site with multiple subjects and topics to explore. This helps with adjusting frequencies and awareness to a higher level, leaving the third dimensional matrix behind.

www.citizenhearing.org On this site you can check into the multiple hearings on disclosing the truth about **UFOs** and us not being alone.

BOOK LIST

Allen, James. (2008, Revised and Updated for the 21st Century) *As a Man Thinketh*. Penguin Group, USA.

Braden, Gregg. (2005, 5th Edition) *The God Code: The Secret of our Past, The promise of our Future*. Hay House Inc. Carlsbad, CA.

Braden, Gregg. (2012, 1st Edition) *Deep Truth: Igniting the Memory of our Origin, History, Destiny, and Fate*. Hay House Inc. Carlsbad, CA.

Braden, Gregg. (2008, 1st Edition) *The Divine Matrix: Bridging Time, Space, Miracles, and Belief*. Hay House Inc. Carlsbad, CA.

Bristol, Claude M. (1991 Edition) *The Magic of Believing*. Pocket Books, New York: Simon & Schuster.

Byrne, Rhonda. (2006) *The Secret*. Beyond Words Publishing. New York: Simon & Schuster.

Campbell, Joseph. *Transformations of Myth through Time: Thirteen brilliant final lectures from the renowned master of mythology*. 1990 by Mythology Limited, Harper & Row, New York.

Campbell, Joseph. (2014, 3rd Edition) *The Hero's Journey: Joseph Campbell on his Life and Work.* (The Collected Works of Joseph Campbell), by Joseph Campbell, Phil Cousineau, et al. New World Library. Novato, CA.

Cannon, Dolores. (1998 Edition) *The Custodians: Beyond Abduction.* Ozark Mountain Publishing Inc. Arkansas.

Cannon, Dolores. (1993, 4th Edition) *Keepers of the Garden.* Ozark Mountain Publishing, Inc. Arkansas, USA.

Cannon, Dolores. (2001 Edition, Book one of Five). *The Convoluted Universe: Book One.* Ozark Mountain Publishing Inc. Arkansas, USA.

Cannon, Dolores. (2011) *The Three Waves of Volunteers & the New Earth.* Ozark Mountain Publishing. Arkansas, USA.

Chopra, Deepak. (1994) *The Seven Spiritual Laws of Success: A practical Guide to the Fulfillment of Your Dreams.* San Rafael, California: Amber-Allen/New World Library.

Coldwell, Dr. Leonard. (2010) *The Only Answer to Tyranny: America's Last Stand.* Liberty House Publishers.

Coldwell, Dr. Leonard. (2010) *The Only Answer to Success: You Were Born to be a Champion.* 21st Century Press.

Cota-Robles, Patricia Diane. (2010) *Who Am I? Why Am I Here?* New Age Study of Humanity's Purpose.

Elkins, Don. – Rueckert, Carla. – McCarty, James. (1984, Book one of Five) *The Ra Material: An Ancient Astronaut Speaks (Law of One)*. L/L Research Group. Louisville, KY.

Emerson, Willis George. (2016 Edition) *The Smoky God: Or, A Voyage to the Inner World*. Create Space Independent Publishing Platform.

Hamilton, Mark. (2012, 3rd Edition) *Neo-Think Super Puzzle: Books 1,2, and 3 in the Same Volume*. I and O Publishing.

Hicks, Esther & Jerry Hicks (The Teachings of Abraham). (2004) *Ask And It Is Given: Learning to Manifest Your Desires*. Carlsbad, California: Hay House.

Hicks, Esther and Jerry. (2009 Edition) *The Vortex: Where the Law of Attraction Assembles All Cooperative Relationships*. Hay House Inc. Carlsbad, CA.

Hill, Napoleon. (2015) *Think and Grow Rich: The Original Version, Restored and Revised*. Mindpower Press.

Hill, Napoleon. (2011) *The Law of Success in Sixteen Lessons: From the 1925 Manuscript Lessons*. Vieux Publishing.

Jaynes, Julian. (2000, 31578th Edition) *The Origin of Consciousness in the Breakdown of the Bicameral Mind.* NY: Houghton Mifflin.

Kahn, Matt. (2016) *Whatever Arises, Love That.* Sounds True, Boulder CO

Lean, Shanna Mac. (2006) *Eternal Twin Flame Love: The Story of Shanna-Pra (Say Yes to Love).* Circle of Light Press.

Mandelker, Scott. (1995) *From Elsewhere: Being E.T. in America.* Carol Publishing Group.

Mandelker, Scott. (2000) *Universal Vision: Soul Evolution and the Cosmic Plan.* UV Way.

Marciniak, Barbara. (1992) *Bringers of the Dawn: Teachings from the Pleiadians.* Bear & Company, Rochester, Vermont.

Newton, Michael. (1994) *Journey of Souls: Case Studies of Life between Lives.* St. Paul, MN: Lllewellyn Publications.

Newton, Michael. (2001) *Destiny of Souls? New Case Studies of Life Between Lives.* St. Paul, MN: Lllewellyn Publications.

Oliver, Frederick S. (2017, Revised 2nd Edition) *A Dweller on two Planets.* Aziloth Books, British Library.

Plummer, Joseph. (2008) *Dishonest Money: Financing the Road to Ruin.* Book-Surge Publishing.

Robbins, Dianne. (2015, Expanded Edition) *Telos: 1st Transmissions Ever Received from the Subterranean City Beneath Mt. Shasta.* Mount Shasta Light Publishing. Mt. Shasta. CA.

Rueckert, Carla L. (2001, 1st Edition) *A Wanderer's Handbook.* L/L Research Group. Louisville, KY.

Stjerna, Mariana. (2018, 2nd Edition) *Agartha: The Earth's Inner World.* Soullink Publishing.

Strassman, Rick. (2001) *DMT: The Spirit Molecule.* Park Street Press, Rochester, Vermont.

Templeton, John Marks. (1998, 1st Edition) *Worldwide Laws of Life: 200 Eternal Spiritual Principles.* Templeton Press.

Tolle, Eckhart. (2005) *A New Earth: Awakening to Your Life's Purpose.* New York: Plume/Penguin.

Tolle, Eckhart. (1999) *The Power of Now: A Guide to Spiritual Enlightenment.* Novato, California: New World Publishing and Vancouver, British Colombia.: Namaste Publishing.

Tonge, Gary. Multiple Authors. (2014 Edition) *The Urantia Book: New and Improved.* Uversa Press Publishing.

Wallace, Frank R. (1972, New Revised Edition) *Poker a Guaranteed Income for Life by Using the Advanced Methods of Poker.* I and O Publishing.

Wallace, Frank R. (1981, #225 Edition) – (Roots Version out of Print) *Neo-Tech: The Neo-Tech Discovery Beyond Cards.* Neo-Tech Publishing.

Wilcock, David. (2014, Reprint Edition) *The Synchronicity Key: The Hidden Intelligence Guiding the Universe and You.* Dutton Publishing.

Wilcock, David. (2012) *The Source Field Investigation: The Hidden Science and Lost Civilizations Behind the 2012 Prophecies.* Dutton Publishing, New York, NY.

Wink, Peter. (2003) *Negotiate Your Way to Riches.* Career Press, Franklin Lakes, NJ.

Ziglar, Zig. (2005, Anniversary Edition) *See You at the Top.* Magna Publishing. Pelican Publishing, Gretna, Louisiana.

NOTE FROM THE AUTHOR

Hello friends! I wanted to inform you about the information I referred you to in the book. All of the recommended material in the book was active and available at the time of this writing. As things change, some material or sites may not be available anymore.

All of the material in the book from websites, books, products…etc., I put in under my own volition. All of these creations and the people bringing them to us deserve recognition for their efforts and all of the material is related to the topics addressed in this book. I am not getting paid by and am not affiliated with any person, business or website in including their material in my book.

I have set up a special email just for the book at:
outofillusion_link@yahoo.com

If you have any questions, comments or you need help finding some material or products, please let me know. I will email you back with the best answers as soon as I can. Thanks for reading and I will talk to you again soon!

In Appreciation

A very special Thank You! to the River Sanctuary Publishing Team. I am grateful for your knowledge and expertise in the publication of this book.

To my Mom, for inspiring me in ways she doesn't even know!

To my friends who have supported me through thick and thin... you know who you are!

To Dr. Leonard Coldwell for mentoring me and helping me bring the champion out in myself!

ABOUT THE AUTHOR

I, the author, Chris Link, was born in Indiana. Through my schooling, I always took a special interest in creative writing, taking advanced courses at the University of Vincennes, in Vincennes, Indiana.

Being a "Late Bloomer," I didn't pursue writing until I became spiritually awake. After my awakening, I began a quest for profound knowledge to become more aware of life and our surroundings. Most of my knowledge comes from self-education through books, audios, online training with special clubs/seminars and dedication/conditioning for success in all areas of life.

I consider these teachings to be spiritually based, but also, general self-growth material for everyone. At the inner core, I believe the message to be about changing our state of awareness. The act of self-transmutation is for all souls to raise their level of love and peace, changing from within their very existence from a low spiritual awareness to a higher one.

It is my wish and goal to help as many people as possible through my writing. In doing so, I am very excited and enthusiastic about this first book to be presented to our beautiful blue planet!

www.ingramcontent.com/pod-product-compliance
Lightning Source LLC
Chambersburg PA
CBHW080500110426
42742CB00017B/2952